IBM Cognos Business Intelligence

Discover the practical approach to BI with
IBM Cognos Business Intelligence

Dustin Adkison

BIRMINGHAM - MUMBAI

IBM Cognos Business Intelligence

First published: May 2013

Production Reference: 1250413

Published by Packt Publishing Ltd.
Livery Place
35 Livery Street
Birmingham B3 2PB, UK.

ISBN 978-1-84968-356-2

www.packtpub.com

Cover Image by Neha Rajappan (neha.rajappan1@gmail.com)

Credits

Author
Dustin Adkison

Reviewers
Brian Green

Andy Rachmiel

Ramin Rahmani

Jeff Wade

Kirk Wiseman

Darshan Donni

Sameer Sheth

Acquisition Editors
Erol Staveley

Edward Gordon

Lead Technical Editor
Mayur Hule

Technical Editors
Sayali Mirajkar

Kaustubh S. Mayekar

Ankita R. Meshram

Copy Editors
Brandt D'Mello

Insiya Morbiwala

Aditya Nair

Alfida Paiva

Project Coordinator
Kranti Berde

Proofreader
Lindsey Thomas

Indexer
Rekha Nair

Production Coordinator
Manu Joseph

Cover Work
Manu Joseph

Foreword

Analytics is proving to be the key for surfacing important insights into business performance and driving improved business outcomes. Organizations that leverage analytics have been shown to significantly outperform their peers. In 2012, when the IBM Institute for Business Value studied the real-world use of big data, 63 percent of those surveyed indicated that the use of information and analytics is creating a competitive advantage for their organizations. What's more interesting is that this figure reflects a 70 percent increase in just the past two years.

Here's a great example of how one company leveraged analytics to transform their business and improve their bottom line. The Cincinnati Zoo & Botanical Garden wanted to optimize the customer experience for their 1.3 million annual visitors, increase attendance, boost sales, and streamline some of their operational processes. With the IBM Business Analytics software and with expertize of IBM Business Partner BrightStar, they were able to create a more accurate 360-degree view of customer behavior that helped increase new visits by 50,000, save the Zoo over $100,000 per year by optimizing promotions and discounts, and increase food revenues by 25 percent over the previous year. These are impressive results driven by greater insight into their data.

For those organizations looking to embed analytics into the fabric of their business, the question becomes: where do I start? The simple answer is by building your skills. That's where the knowledge from books like this one will help.

This book will help new users of IBM Cognos Business Intelligence to quickly learn the analytics skills—from basic usage to advanced authoring—to communicate analytics to people across the organization. Those individuals who are upgrading from IBM Cognos Business Intelligence Version 8 will learn more about the new features in this release. This technology is putting more power in the hands of users throughout the organization to create their own reports and do their own analysis—which greatly reduces the reliance on IT departments.

Additionally, in this book you will get step-by-step how-to information for the different components of IBM Cognos Business Intelligence, and how end users, business users, and developers/administrators would use these features. This book will help you learn how to use BI tools to deliver business intelligence to users wherever they are—in their office, on mobile devices, or offline.

Improving your organization's **Analytics Quotient (AQ)** will complement the technical skills in your analytics journey. Evaluating your AQ will help you understand how well you're using analytics now and guide you to that next step in analytics growth. Assess your Analytics Quotient now by taking IBM's AQ quiz.

There's no question that the speed of business continues to accelerate. What's good to see is that the power of technology is not only keeping pace but also providing the tools to steer the business towards better results. In the analytics space, the even better news is that users throughout an organization are in the driver's seat—having the tools at their fingertips to gain insight from information.

Gene Villeneuve
Director, Product Management, Interactive Analytics & BI
Business Analytics
IBM

About the Author

Dustin Adkison is an active member of the IBM Cognos community. He began his career in Business Intelligence at one of the premier Cognos customers, BlueCross BlueShield of Tennessee. After a short period, he became one of the Cognos administrators of a very large Cognos implementation as well as the training coordinator for all Cognos needs. While at BCBST, Dustin began to shape his skills in Cognos Report, which later became IBM Cognos 8 and IBM Cognos 10.

Dustin soon joined the Cognos consulting industry with Market Street Solutions (a Tennessee-based IBM Premier Partner that focuses on IBM Cognos). There he worked as both a consultant and a sales and presales resource. Dustin was an active member of the Atlanta and Tennessee Cognos User Groups during this time. He also further developed his skills around IBM Cognos and began presenting to various user communities.

For the last 5 years, Dustin has worked for BrightStar Partners and BSP Software, which are now owned by Avnet. He manages a team of sales resources, provides sales and technical sales support, and sets the direction for the sales team. Dustin is currently an active member of the Wisconsin, Illinois, Indiana, St. Louis, and Michigan User Groups. He has been a speaker at each of these User Groups in the past. In addition, he has presented at the Chattanooga, Nashville, Cincinnati, Columbus, Victoria, Toronto, and Vancouver User Groups as a guest.

As one of the leaders of the adoption of Cognos Express, Dustin was asked to present both on a panel and as an individual at IBM **Information on Demand (IOD)** and on a `cfo.com` webcast. Dustin has written about the importance of soft skills in the BI industry and has had his writings featured on various forums.

For the past two years, Dustin has been honored as an IBM Champion, an award that is given to the information leaders within the IBM space.

Acknowledgement

I would like to thank my content editors/reviewers: Brian Green, Andy Rachmiel, Ramin Rahmani, Jeff Wade, and Kirk Wiseman. I appreciate each of you for not being afraid to call out my mistakes and, in doing so, helping me to learn and grow. For all of you, that is true not only in this writing, but in my career and the growth of it that you have each helped to shape.

I would like to thank my co-workers who have helped me to learn much of what I have shared in this book. Many of you helped mentor me at BlueCross BlueShield of Tennessee and at Market Street Solutions. Many of you have taught me new techniques at BSP. It is through teaming together that we can each hope to grow our skills the most.

Finally, I would like to thank my family and friends for supporting me while I was writing this book. You have all been a huge emotional support with the constant encouragement. I especially would like to thank my loving wife, Amanda. I know that this has required almost as much sacrifice from you as it has from me. Thank you for all of the weekends, where you have taken care of things that I would normally help with so that I could have time to write. I could not do anything without you. I love you.

About the Reviewers

Brian Green is the manager of Business Intelligence and Performance Management at BlueCross BlueShield of Tennessee. He has over 30 years of experience in Information Management and has co-authored two books about developing successful Business Intelligence and Analytics programs.

Andy Rachmiel is the VP of Software Solutions, Business Analytics at BSP Software, an Avnet Services company. He's a high octane, laser-focused, and highly entrepreneurial individual that exudes passion and integrity in all aspects of his life. Andy leads by example and lives for the challenge. Over the past decade Andy built and ran very successful consulting and software companies. Both BrightStar Partners and BSP Software were acquired in 2012 by Avnet, Inc.

Ramin Rahmani focuses on delivering end-to-end Data warehouse, analysis, and reporting solutions that meet business needs. Ramin builds strong relationships through trust and workable business/technical strategies, which shape many successful IBM Cognos BI and BSP Software clients in Australia. Ramin specializes in IBM Cognos and WhereScape data warehouse and business intelligence tools. He has managed multiple successful consultancies and has over a decade of experience as a highly-sought-after consultant covering Australia.

Jeff Wade is the CEO and president of Market Street Solutions, a Business Analytics solutions firm based in Chattanooga, Tennessee. He has over 30 years of experience helping enterprise clients leverage technology to improve their business performance. Jeff's company, Market Street Solutions, has been recognized multiple times on the Inc. 5000 list of fastest growing companies, Business TN's Fast 50, and as an IBM Premier Business Partner.

Kirk Wiseman is the president of PerformanceG2, an IBM Premier partner that specializes in Business Analytics. Kirk has over 15 years experience in the information technology industry with an emphasis in Business Analytics, specifically with Cognos, where he spent over eight years of his career supporting the North and South American Cognos user base as a trainer, consultant, and architect. Kirk came to PerformanceG2 from Merador, where he was the Director of Training Services. Prior to Merador, Kirk was a trainer and consultant at Cognos Corporation, where he was recognized with awards including North American trainer of the year and Eclipse Outstanding Performance. In addition, Kirk was a Program Director at ITI, a private post-graduate school located throughout Canada. Kirk holds a Bachelor of Science degree from Memorial University of Newfoundland and a Post Graduate diploma in Applied Information Technology from ITI.

Kirk contributes Business Analytics videos to YouTube on a regular basis that can be viewed at `http://www.youtube.com/PerformanceG2` and blogs at `http://www.performanceg2.com/blog`. You can contact Kirk at `kirk.wiseman@performanceg2.com`.

I would like to thank Dustin for putting together this book and Packt for giving me the opportunity to review. I hope my feedback proved helpful. Much love and thanks for my wife, Mireille, and our three children: Aiden, Zachary and Kaelyn.

Darshan Donni has worked with the Cognos BI third-level support team in the IBM India Software Labs. Prior to this, he worked with the Cognos BI second-level support team. He blogged actively on `http://cognoscommentary.blogspot.com`. He has participated in numerous customer engagements for IBM clients.

Sameer Sheth has been practicing as a Business Intelligence and Data Warehousing consultant since the year 2004. His primary focus is on architectural design and development and implementation of Enterprise Performance Management, Business Intelligence and Data Warehousing solutions across various domains, such as oil and gas, the education sector, retail, financial spectrum, health care, and airline industries.

Overall he has more than 13 years of relevant experience in the IT industry blended with proven project management skills. His key roles have been that of a Senior Implementation Lead, a Senior Solution Architect, and a Project Manager. He has also spent time as a Technical Mentor.

Sameer is certified in Global Business Leadership from Harvard Business School Publishing, USA. Along with it, he is certified in Managerial Excellence from Duke University Fuqua School of Business, USA. He has earned numerous IBM certifications including IBM Certified Solution Designer—Cognos 10 Planning, IBM Certified Solution Expert—Cognos 8 Planning, and IBM Certified Solution Designer—Cognos 8 Planning.

Sameer has been the technical reviewer for few books published by Packt Publishing, such as *IBM Cognos TM1 Developer's Certification Guide* and *IBM Cognos Business Intelligence 10.1 Dashboarding Cookbook*. This book was developed for users to successfully understand, implement, and obtain the best ROI on their Business Intelligence solution.

Heartfelt thanks to my wife Shruthi for a lifetime of endless patience, love, and support.

www.PacktPub.com

Support files, eBooks, discount offers and more

You might want to visit www.PacktPub.com for support files and downloads related to your book.

Did you know that Packt offers eBook versions of every book published, with PDF and ePub files available? You can upgrade to the eBook version at www.PacktPub.com and as a print book customer, you are entitled to a discount on the eBook copy. Get in touch with us at service@packtpub.com for more details.

At www.PacktPub.com, you can also read a collection of free technical articles, sign up for a range of free newsletters and receive exclusive discounts and offers on Packt books and eBooks.

http://PacktLib.PacktPub.com

Do you need instant solutions to your IT questions? PacktLib is Packt's online digital book library. Here, you can access, read and search across Packt's entire library of books.

Why Subscribe?

- Fully searchable across every book published by Packt
- Copy and paste, print and bookmark content
- On demand and accessible via web browser

Free Access for Packt account holders

If you have an account with Packt at www.PacktPub.com, you can use this to access PacktLib today and view nine entirely free books. Simply use your login credentials for immediate access.

Instant Updates on New Packt Books

Get notified! Find out when new books are published by following @PacktEnterprise on Twitter, or the *Packt Enterprise* Facebook page.

Table of Contents

Preface

IBM Cognos Business Intelligence is a reporting and analytics product that enables end users to develop robust reports and analyses through a web interface. This book will look at the latest version of IBM Cognos BI, IBM Cognos BI V10. With the release of IBM Cognos BI V10, we find many new features, such as:

- IBM Cognos Workspace — a self-service dashboard and collaboration area
- IBM Cognos Workspace Advanced — a tool for creating ad hoc reports and analyses that are of a high quality and are flexible
- Native support for more mobile devices
- Active Reports — IBM Cognos BI reports that store data for offline consumption of information
- Many more new features within the existing framework

In this book we will look at the new features that come with IBM Cognos BI V10, and we will also revisit the features that were available in earlier versions of Cognos BI.

What this book covers

Chapter 1, IBM Cognos Connection, covers the IBM Cognos Business Intelligence Cognos Connection interface that is accessed by end users and developers. Cognos Connection is the default web interface for navigating IBM Cognos Business Intelligence V10. This chapter covers in detail some of the common ways in which end users interact with this web interface.

Chapter 2, Introducing IBM Cognos Workspace, covers the new self-service dashboard tool in IBM Cognos Business Intelligence that allows end users to create their own interactive dashboards. This chapter covers in detail how to add content to Cognos Workspace, how to filter that content, and how to change the way content is viewed.

Chapter 3, IBM Cognos Active Reports, covers how end users interact with Cognos Active Reports. Cognos Active reports are MHT files that contain data and formatting information in a single file. As such, they are easy to take with you on your laptop or a mobile device.

Chapter 4, IBM Cognos Mobile, covers how to interact with IBM Cognos Business Intelligence on a mobile device. This chapter covers in detail how to access mobile content and interact with it on an Apple iPad.

Chapter 5, IBM Cognos Query Studio, covers the legacy product, Cognos Query Studio. Although IBM Cognos Workspace Advanced is the preferred product for creating ad hoc reports, many environments will still have Cognos Query Studio installed. This chapter shows in detail how to create a simple report using Cognos Query Studio.

Chapter 6, IBM Cognos Analysis Studio, covers the legacy product, Cognos Analysis Studio. Although IBM Cognos Workspace Advanced is the preferred product for performing basic analysis, many environments will still have Cognos Analysis Studio installed. This chapter shows in detail how to create a simple analysis using Cognos Analysis Studio.

Chapter 7, IBM Cognos Workspace Advanced, covers the new tool, Cognos Workspace Advanced. Cognos Workspace Advanced allows basic developers to create high-quality reports and analyses in one interface. It also interacts directly with Cognos Workspace for a seamless, single interface. This chapter covers in detail how to create new reports and analyses using Cognos Workspace Advanced.

Chapter 8, IBM Cognos Report Studio, covers how to create complex reports using Cognos Report Studio. Cognos Report Studio is the most powerful and complex development tool within IBM Cognos Business Intelligence. This chapter shows in detail how to create reports using this incredibly powerful tool.

Chapter 9, IBM Cognos Framework Manager, covers the metadata design tool for IBM Cognos Business Intelligence. This tool allows you to change how data is displayed, how to create custom calculation and model table relationships, and so much more. This chapter shows in detail how to create a simple model using Cognos Framework Manager.

Chapter 10, Administration and Performance Tuning, covers the basics of how to administer IBM Cognos Business Intelligence and some common tips on performance tuning for your environment.

Chapter 11, Common Administrator Tasks – Streamlined, covers Avnet's BSP Software product offerings. These offerings are add-ons to IBM Cognos Business Intelligence that help to enhance the product.

Chapter 12, User Adoption, covers ideas for how to increase user adoption. The greatest product in the world will still need users to make it successful. This chapter shows in detail, tips and tricks for creating your user community into IBM Cognos Business Intelligence.

What you need for this book

In order to make the most of this book, you need to have an environment set up with IBM Cognos Business Intelligence V10. This book does not cover installation and configuration; however, Cognos Business Intelligence does ship with a detailed installation and configuration guide that can be used for assistance.

Who this book is for

This book is designed for administrators, developers, end users, and other stakeholders working with IBM Cognos Business Intelligence V10.

Conventions

In this book, you will find a number of styles of text that distinguish between different kinds of information. Here are some examples of these styles, and an explanation of their meaning.

Code words in text, database table names, folder names, filenames, file extensions, pathnames, dummy URLs, user input, and Twitter handles are shown as follows: "For instance, a set of folders structured this way may be named `Financial Data`, `Sales Information`, or `Marketing Results`."

New terms and **important words** are shown in bold. Words that you see on the screen, in menus or dialog boxes for example, appear in the text like this: "Report views, on the other hand, are created from within the **Actions** area for the report for which you are creating a view".

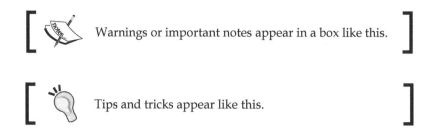

Warnings or important notes appear in a box like this.

Tips and tricks appear like this.

Reader feedback

Feedback from our readers is always welcome. Let us know what you think about this book—what you liked or may have disliked. Reader feedback is important for us to develop titles that you really get the most out of.

To send us general feedback, simply send an e-mail to feedback@packtpub.com, and mention the book title via the subject of your message.

If there is a topic that you have expertise in and you are interested in either writing or contributing to a book, see our author guide on www.packtpub.com/authors.

Customer support

Now that you are the proud owner of a Packt book, we have a number of things to help you to get the most from your purchase.

Errata

Although we have taken every care to ensure the accuracy of our content, mistakes do happen. If you find a mistake in one of our books—maybe a mistake in the text or the code—we would be grateful if you would report this to us. By doing so, you can save other readers from frustration and help us improve subsequent versions of this book. If you find any errata, please report them by visiting http://www.packtpub. com/submit-errata, selecting your book, clicking on the **errata submission form** link, and entering the details of your errata. Once your errata are verified, your submission will be accepted and the errata will be uploaded on our website, or added to any list of existing errata, under the Errata section of that title. Any existing errata can be viewed by selecting your title from http://www.packtpub.com/support.

Piracy

Piracy of copyright material on the Internet is an ongoing problem across all media. At Packt, we take the protection of our copyright and licenses very seriously. If you come across any illegal copies of our works, in any form, on the Internet, please provide us with the location address or website name immediately so that we can pursue a remedy.

Please contact us at copyright@packtpub.com with a link to the suspected pirated material.

We appreciate your help in protecting our authors, and our ability to bring you valuable content.

Questions

You can contact us at questions@packtpub.com if you are having a problem with any aspect of the book, and we will do our best to address it.

1
IBM Cognos Connection

IBM Cognos Connection is the out-of-the-box interface that IBM provides with IBM Cognos Business Intelligence. It is the primary interface for finding reports, opening development studios, and collaborating with other users within your business intelligence environment. IBM Cognos Connection was first introduced with **Cognos ReportNet** (**CRN**), but it is worth revisiting here in order to set the stage for the rest of the book.

In this chapter, we will look at the concept of web-based reporting, talk about the customizations that are available, and explore the interface, that is, IBM Cognos Connection. Some of the areas that we will look at are:

- Web-based reporting
- The welcome page
- Folder structures
- My Area
- Searching
- Running reports
- Scheduling reports
- Cutting, copying, pasting, and deleting objects
- Creating URLs, jobs, and report views
- The business case for IBM Cognos Connection

Web-based reporting

If you were to follow the evolution of reporting, you would find a logical transition that shows companies uncovering as much information as they could in as meaningful a way as possible while using the best technology available.

In the 1980s, the key concepts of reporting were defined and enhanced. Companies were learning how to use computers to make decisions based on their data. Reports were built from software tools that resided on end user computers. The tools would connect to company databases for reporting purposes. Later, the data would be consolidated into OLAP (or cube) data sources for reporting. OLAP stands for Online Analytics Processing and is a standard term to used describe data that is formatted for multidimensional analysis. With OLAP, data is preconsolidated with multiple cross-sections of data. This allows for faster reporting.

In the late 1990s, during the dot-com boom, software was developed to bring reporting into the Web. Cognos ReportNet was one of the first tools to do so. Much of the technology introduced by this tool remains as the backbone of Cognos BI today.

With the introduction of web-based reporting, users around the world could share one centralized version of their data. All data and reports began to be stored in a single location, which made it easier to manage the information that was being dispersed within and outside an organization.

A few key benefits of web-based reporting are:

- Centralization of information
- Ease of management, maintenance, and administration
- Minimization of IT overhead
- Improved data security

IBM Cognos Business Intelligence v10.x continues to use the web-based platform that was developed for Cognos ReportNet. Let's start by taking a look at the welcome screen that many users see when they first log on to IBM Cognos BI v10.x via the Web.

The welcome page

The welcome screen is designed to help steer new users towards the tool that will meet their need for reporting or analytics. Most users will eventually choose to not show the welcome screen at start-up, simply because it can slow you down from getting to the report or report design tool that you are interested in accessing.

This is how the welcome screen appears:

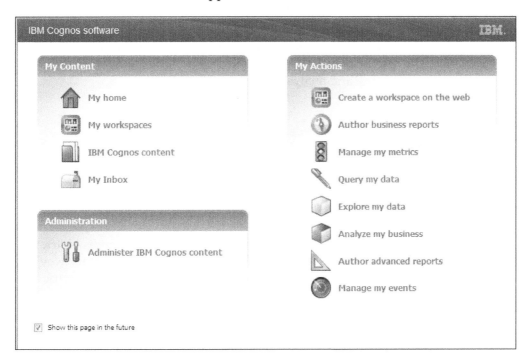

You can see from the preceding screenshot that there are a variety of options available. The options shown on the screen will be determined by the access rights that are defined for each user and the options that have been installed by the administrator. For the purpose of this book, we will have administrator access, which will allow us to see every available option.

The available options are as follows:

- **My Content** options:
    - ° **My home**: This option will take a user to their defined home page, which they can set by setting any area as their default.
    - ° **My dashboards**: This option will load Cognos Workspace along with options to load saved dashboard views.

- ° **IBM Cognos content**: This option will take you to the **Public Folders** area. **Public Folders** is a place where shared content is stored.

- ° **My Inbox**: This option will take a user to the **My Inbox** area. The **My Inbox** area allows users to set and assign tasks related to reporting and analysis.

- **My Actions** options:

  - ° **Create my dashboards**: This option will take you to Cognos Workspace and will allow you to create a new Cognos Workspace dashboard.

  - ° **Author business reports**: This option will take you to Cognos Workspace Advanced, which will allow you to create business reports and analyses.

  - ° **Manage my metrics**: This option will take you to Cognos Metric Studio. In Cognos Metric Studio, you can manage and track **Key Performance Indicators (KPI)** for your business. Cognos Metric Studio is outside the scope of this book.

  - ° **Query my data**: This option will take you to Cognos Query Studio. Cognos Query Studio allows you to create standard report queries.

  - ° **Explore my data**: This option will launch Cognos PowerPlay Studio. Cognos PowerPlay Studio is a legacy tool that was carried over from IBM Cognos Series 7 PowerPlay web. Cognos PowerPlay Studio is outside the scope of this book.

  - ° **Analyze my business**: This option will launch Cognos Analysis Studio. Cognos Analysis Studio is an interface that allows you to perform data discovery with OLAP: preaggregated data.

  - ° **Author advanced reports**: This option will launch Cognos Report Studio. Cognos Report Studio is the primary report development interface in IBM Cognos BI. Cognos Report Studio allows you to create very advanced reports.

  - ° **Manage my events**: This option will launch Cognos Event Studio. Cognos Event Studio allows monitoring of data based on data triggers. You can set up data-based triggers that can do anything from starting a process to sending an e-mail.

- The **Administration** option:
  - ○ **Administer IBM Cognos content**: This option will launch the IBM Cognos Administration interface. This is where you can do everything from tracking the status of your IBM Cognos BI environment to setting up data source connections to manage security.

- The **Quick tour** option:
  - ○ The **Quick tour** area has overviews for IBM Cognos Connection and each of the studios. These are useful, high-level overviews for end users who are new to IBM Cognos BI v10.x.

Folder structures

The default folder structure will have two primary folders that can be viewed within the two default tabs in IBM Cognos Connection (**Public Folders** and **My Folders)**. **Public Folders** is where shared content is stored, whereas **My Folders** is more for personal content. The default screen that can be seen is as follows:

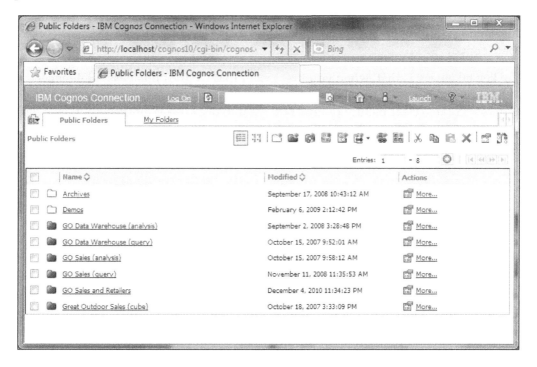

In the preceding screenshot, you can also see two types of folders. The yellow folders (the first two in the screenshot) represent purely structural folders that hold content. The blue folders (third folder onwards in this example) represent packages.

A **package** is a set of metadata that defines how IBM Cognos BI will query a data source. The metadata may define things such as formatting of data from the database, or it could have more advanced calculations for data from the database before it is presented to the end users in IBM Cognos BI.

The way that you choose to structure these folders will depend on your environment. Many businesses choose to structure the folders based on the data that is contained within them. For instance, a set of folders structured this way may be named `Financial Data`, `Sales Information`, or `Marketing Results`. A second alternative would be to structure the folders by functional areas of the business. In this scenario, you may use folder names such as `Human Resources`, `Marketing`, or `Accounting`. For the purpose of this section, a third and final way of structuring the folders would be by cost center or team. This tends to be the most granular way of structuring the folders and will often require replication of packages into multiple folders. You can use this folder-structure model in conjunction with the functional-areas model and have subfolders named after each group or team within a department. Examples of this naming convention may include folders such as `Bob's Team`, `Web Support`, or `Cost Center 1234`.

The key takeaway is that, when you first install IBM Cognos Business Intelligence v10.x, you will have a blank slate. It is easy to simply begin creating packages and folders without a clear picture of how you want to organize your content. However, if you plan ahead, you can have a much cleaner and easier way to navigate the content environment for your end users.

My Area

IBM Cognos BI allows the end users to separate out their personal items and preferences from the shared ones. This is done through **My Folders**, as discussed in the previous section, but it can also be done in My Area. The My Area option is shown as a little avatar icon that will allow users to interact with areas and set preferences that are unique to them.

From within My Area, you can access **My Inbox**. **My Inbox** is new with IBM Cognos Business Intelligence v10.x and is an interface for setting and managing tasks related to Cognos development.

My Watch Items will allow users to interact with alerts and rules that they have set on specific data points within different reports. Watch items are data points on reports that users want to track. This can be done by right-clicking on a data point within a report and choosing to watch for changes. As an end user, you can then set thresholds to alert you of changes made. In the **My Watch Items** area, you can edit and remove these alerts and rules.

An end user can customize the look and feel of their Cognos BI environment through the **My Preferences** area under My Area as well. The **My Preference** area looks like the following screenshot:

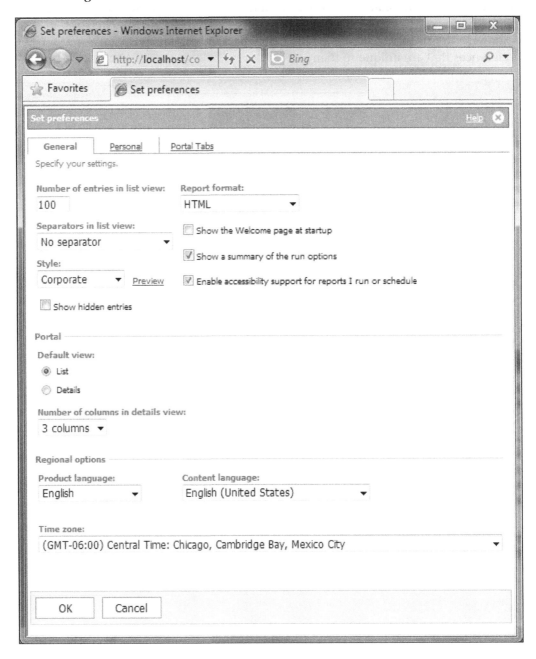

Within this **My Preferences** area, you can set a number of variables:

- **Number of entries in list view**: This field will tell IBM Cognos BI how many items to show when navigating folders. The default is 15, but that will often cause users to have to scroll between the pages of content. I recommend setting this to a higher number.

- **Report format**: This field will allow you to choose the default report format when a report is run. The options available are **HTML**, **PDF**, **Excel 2007**, **Excel 2007 data**, **Excel 2002**, **Delimited text (CSV)**, and **XML**.

- **Separators in list view**: This field will allow you to set line separators. The options available are **Grid lines**, **alternating backgrounds**, and **no gridlines**.

- **Style**: This field will determine the IBM Cognos BI style that is used for the entire interface. There are a number of default styles available, but custom styles can be set here as well. These styles can change the color schemes, images, and formatting of the Cognos Connection environment.

- The check box options:
    - **Show the Welcome page at startup**: This option will let you choose whether or not to start on the welcome page when logging in.
    - **Show a summary of the run options**: This option will show a summary of the run options selected for reports that are run in batches.
    - **Enable accessibility support for reports I run or schedule**: This option will allow separate text for users with special needs.
    - **Show hidden entries**: This is a feature that administrators can choose to not give to all users. It will allow users to see a faded icon for items that have been marked as hidden.

- **Portal** options include:
    - The **Default view** options are:
        List: This option will provide a list of objects without details

        Details: This option will allow you to see more details about each object
    - **Number of columns in details view**: The more columns you choose, the more details you will see in the Cognos Connection portal

- **Regional options** include:
  - ○ **Product language**: This will let you choose the language that the IBM Cognos BI interface uses.
  - ○ **Content language**: This will allow you to choose a default language for the content within your reports. This feature requires a locale to be set for the language chosen for the report content.
  - ○ **Time zone**: This will allow you to select your default time zone.

My Activities and Schedules will allow you to view and manage all of your scheduled reports and activities through one interface.

My Recycle Bin is an add-on product from BSP Software that allows users to recover deleted content. Administrators can control how long to keep items in the recycle bin and can restore any user's content from the **Administration** area. The end user interface looks like the following screenshot:

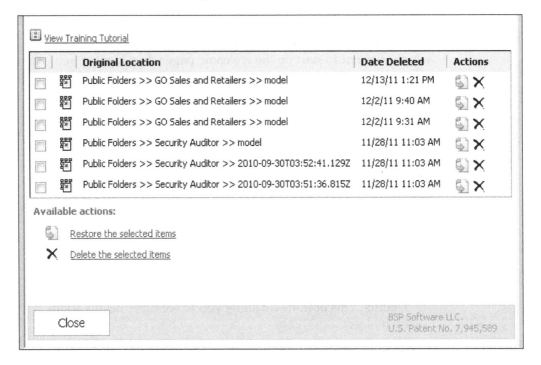

Searching

Searching has evolved since it was first introduced in ReportNet. The searching capability that is available in IBM Cognos BI v10.x is the equivalent of the Go! Search functionality that was available in IBM Cognos BI v8.x. The way it works is pretty simple. From the **Administration** area, you can create a search index for your content. With this new search, you can search the report content as well as the metadata for the reports. Previously, searching would only search names and descriptions of the content.

Running reports

Running existing reports can be done in a couple of different ways. For reports that do not have saved output, you can run the report to the default output format by simply clicking on it. The more advanced way to run a report would be to use **Run with options** by clicking the blue play icon highlighted in the following screenshot:

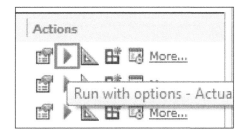

Once within the **Run with options** area, you will see a variety of options that relate to the formatting, accessibility, language, delivery method, and prompt entry for the report.

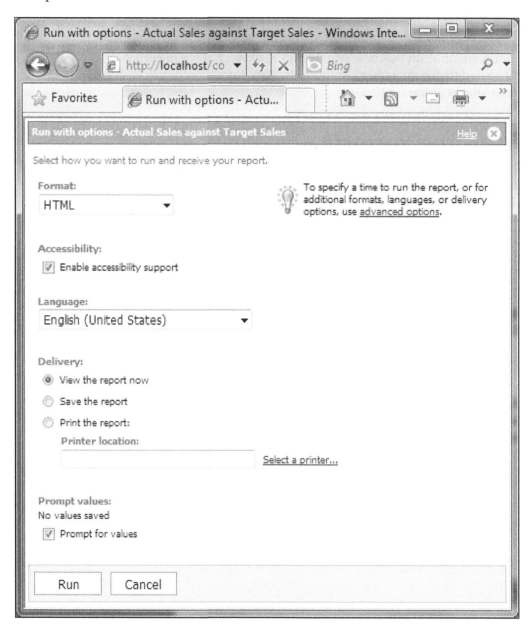

The **Format, Accessibility**, and **Language** options are the same options that can be set as defaults within the **My Preferences** area. The **Delivery** option allows a user to determine how they will receive the report. The most commonly available options (not all shown here) are:

- **View the report now**: This option will bring the report to the end user once it is done running. It will run live against the underlying data source.

- **Save the report**: This option will save the report output to be viewed later. If this option is selected and **advanced options** is also selected, you can choose multiple report outputs and delivery methods for the report that is run. You can then open the saved report outputs without having to reaccess the data source.

- **Print the report**: This option will allow you to print to any printer on the network that has been set up within IBM Cognos BI.

- **Save to file system** (not shown): This option will allow you to save the report output to a file system as defined within IBM Cognos Configuration.

- **Deliver to a mobile device** (not shown): This option will allow you to push the report to a mobile device.

- **Send the report by email** (not shown): This option will allow you to e-mail the report to a recipient.

The **advanced options** interface, as seen in the following screenshot, allows an end user to select multiple outputs and delivery methods. It also allows for scheduling a one-time run of a report for a future time.

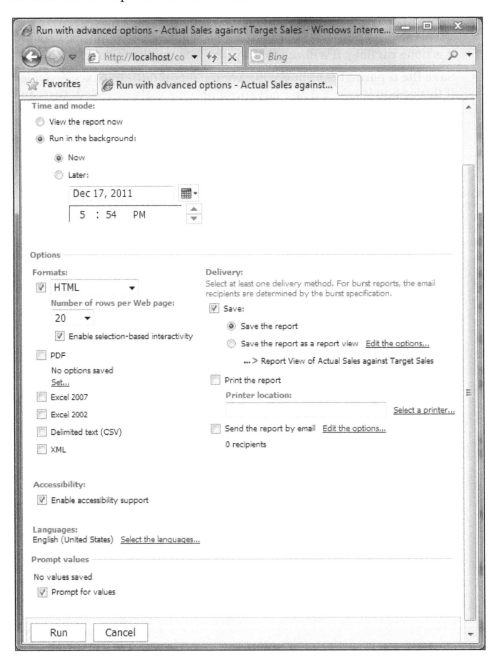

The interface is very similar for scheduling; however, **Run with options** is designed for a one-time run of a report. The scheduling interface is designed for repeated report runs.

Scheduling reports

Reports are often scheduled in situations where data is changing at specific intervals. Scheduled reports can be delivered via the same mechanisms as that for the **Run with options** reports. The only difference is that, with scheduled reports, IBM Cognos BI provides frequency options that can be set. You can access the scheduling interface via the icon that looks like a calendar (highlighted with a square in the following screenshot):

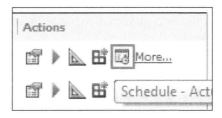

The additional section for setting frequency can be seen in the following screenshot:

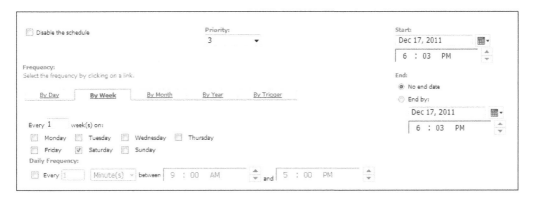

This interface let's you set the priority for a schedule in case it is competing with other schedules. It will also let you set a frequency for your report to run. You can run the report within the day (down to the minute), by week (for certain days during the week), by month (for certain days of the month or on certain days of the week in specific weeks of the month), by year, or by triggers that are taking place within your data. You can also set the start and end times for the report to run.

Cutting, copying, pasting, and deleting objects

Within IBM Cognos Connection, there are options for copying, cutting, and pasting content between folders. This can be useful if you want to reorganize the structure of your environment, create duplicates of the content in additional folders or in your **My Folders** area, or if you want to clean up an environment. These three icons are depicted in the following screenshot:

The scissors are for cutting, the two pieces of paper are for copying, the clipboard is for pasting, and **X** is for deleting.

Creating URLs, jobs, and report views

Most true end users do not build reports or analyses but simply consume prebuilt content. However, as an end user you are able to create new content. The content that you can create will typically be URLs, jobs, or report views.

- **URLs**: These will allow you to link to any web address from within IBM Cognos Connection.

- **Jobs**: A job is a group of reports that are all scheduled to run together. These can be run with the same run options or you can set individual run options for each report. You can also choose whether to run these in sequence or all at once.

- **Report views**: These are views of the prompted reports that have the prompt values already set. This keeps you from having to re-enter the prompt values each time you re-run a report.

URLs and jobs are both created from the menu bar in IBM Cognos Connection. The icons for the tasks are shown in the following screenshot:

As shown in the preceding screenshot, the icon with the two gears is the job icon, and the icon with the globe and a link symbol is the URL icon.

Report views on the other hand are created from within the **Actions** area of the report for which you are creating a view. You can create a new report view by clicking on the icon highlighted in the following screenshot:

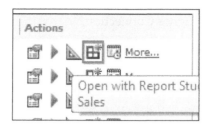

The business case for Cognos

After understanding all of the technical details behind IBM Cognos Connection, you have to ask yourself why your business users will want this. There are really a few key reasons.

The first is that, by having IBM Cognos Connection as a central source of data and information, your business users do not risk having different Business Intelligence interfaces providing dissimilar information. This is one version of the truth. The benefit really lies in the ability of the business to trust their numbers.

The second benefit is the ease of use. By having all of your reporting, analysis, and planning tools in one centralized location, business users can more easily complete their work. Because the interfaces are similar between each of the tools, there is also a shared learning experience that would not exist if the tools were all spread between distinct systems.

The third and final benefit that we will discuss here is the ease of support. While it is easy to see this as an IT benefit, and not a business benefit, it is actually a benefit to both groups. For the business, having one interface that is maintained means that support issues can all go to one place. With IBM Cognos BI v10.x, you typically see one group owning the product in its entirety. This means one throat to choke, so to speak.

In reality, there are thousands of business cases that can be drawn around a centralized interface for business analytics. However, these are just a few of the key ones that can help IT better understand why business users should be all for Cognos Connection.

Summary

So far, we have looked at the IBM Cognos Connection interface that an end user would interact with. This interface is geared toward navigating and finding prebuilt content that consists of reports, analyses, and other useful information. As an end user, you can customize the look and feel of your Cognos Connection experience, run and schedule reports, and create new objects such as URLs and report views. We also took a look at the business case for using Cognos Connection.

In the next chapter, we will look at an interface designed for more advanced end user consumption through dashboards called Cognos Workspace.

2
Introducing IBM Cognos Workspace

Cognos Workspace is a self-service dashboard tool that was developed and first released with IBM Cognos Business Intelligence v10.2. Cognos Workspace is web-based and can be accessed through IBM Cognos Connection. It is designed to allow the end users to build their own dashboards without the help of IT.

In this chapter, we will discuss how to add content to the dashboard, filter the content, change the formatting of the content, add comments to the content, and share the content. We will also look at the types of end users that are most likely to use Cognos Workspace and what the business benefits of this tool include.

The topics covered in this chapter include:

- The Self-service dashboard
- Adding content and content types
- Filtering
- Changing the formatting
- Sharing the dashboard
- The business case for Cognos Workspace

The self-service dashboard

A self-service dashboard is a tool that puts the power into the hands of the end users and allows them to bring data, which is most important for their business needs, into one centralized location. To fully understand what a self-service dashboard is, we need to start with the understanding of what a dashboard is.

A standard dashboard is a collection of graphical and numeric information all brought together on one screen or page. With IBM Cognos Business Intelligence, the idea has always been that it needs to be interactive data, or otherwise a dashboard loses some of its power. You may be asking yourself, how to interact with data? There are a few typically used ways of making a dashboard interactive. Drill-down, drill-through, links to the metrics, links to the other systems, hover-over, or comment capabilities are a few of the most commonly used techniques. The following is a brief overview of each:

- **Drill-down** is a mechanism of clicking on a piece of information and seeing the next level below that information in some sort of a hierarchy (for example, click on a country and see a list of states within the country). Drill-down is useful for information having multiple levels of data that need to be compared to one another only within the context of their group within a level. For instance, if I continued to drill from a country down to a state, down to a city, I will only be seeing cities for the state that I click on. If it makes sense to compare those cities to the cities in other states, then drill-down is likely not the mechanism that you will want to use.

- **Drill-through** is a mechanism for going from one view of the information to another view of the information that is either at a lower level within the hierarchy or contains additional information about the object selected. Similar to the drill down mechanism, you are moving to the next level of the hierarchy, but you are changing how the information is presented. A good example of a drill-through would be clicking on something that is summarized, in a chart for instance, and having a new window open with details regarding what you clicked on. The drill-through mechanisms are most useful when you are done reviewing the summarized information, and you are ready to get down to the specifics.

- **Metric** is a single measuring point by which a company or a group of people within a company choose to measure success over time. Metrics are typically presented as goals and actuals and are very commonly shown as red, yellow, or green indicators of success. A dashboard will often contain metrics without any details. Within Cognos Business Intelligence, by clicking on a metric, you can launch Metric Studio and begin understanding how metrics relate to one another, and in turn begin to understand the areas of your business that are driving your results.

- A link is the same thing that you would see anywhere on the Web. Since Cognos Business Intelligence v10.x is web-based, links can be embedded within reports to make them more interactive. What's really cool is that you can even pass information from Cognos Business Intelligence into your links in order to dynamically determine where your links take you. A good example of this would be if you were reporting on the call-center information and you wanted to link to the call-center support ticket in a separate ticketing system. With Cognos Business Intelligence, you could display details on a report and provide dynamic links that would automatically pass the ticket number as a parameter to the ticket system. The end result will be that when you click the link, it opens up the ticket that you clicked on.

- **Hover-over** is a mechanism for providing additional information when a user rests the mouse pointer over a set of data. This is commonly used on charts where you do not want to display all numbers on the chart, but you still want users to be able to see the exact numbers if they choose to. The hover-over mechanism will typically contain details that are not essential for understanding the information presented. In some cases, a chart that simply makes it clear that the numbers have changed and relatively how much they have changed is enough. However, it never hurts to provide a quick mechanism for viewing the details behind the charts.

- A comment is a user-annotated piece of information. Comments are essentially used for fully understanding the information. A good example would be if you are looking at a chart of sales numbers, and you see that a division of your sales team had sold 25 percent less than the previous quarter. If a manager of that sales team has the ability to comment, they can add a comment (typically using the hover-over style) that explains why the sales were down. As an executive, this is helpful to have the holistic view of the information (both, captured quantitative data and entered qualitative data) in one centralized place.

With that brief background and overview of some of the techniques used in dashboards, we can now look at what a self-service dashboard is. A self-service dashboard is a collection of graphical and numeric information that you build for yourself. In Cognos Business Intelligence, you build the dashboard from the queries that already exist somewhere on a report. You, as the end user, can take the elements from the existing reports and drag them onto your dashboard. You can also add filters, change formatting, add comments, and share the final version of your dashboard.

By taking the developed dashboard and pushing it out to the end user, an organization can save the time of their developers, allow their end users greater flexibility, and create a faster transfer of information.

We will now look at the Cognos Workspace interface and some of the most common activities that you and your end users will need to learn to perform.

In order to access Cognos Workspace and begin building a new dashboard right from the welcome screen, click on **Create my dashboards** as shown in the following screenshot:

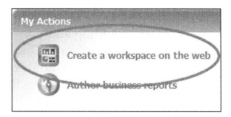

This will bring you to the Cognos Workspace splash screen as shown in the following screenshot:

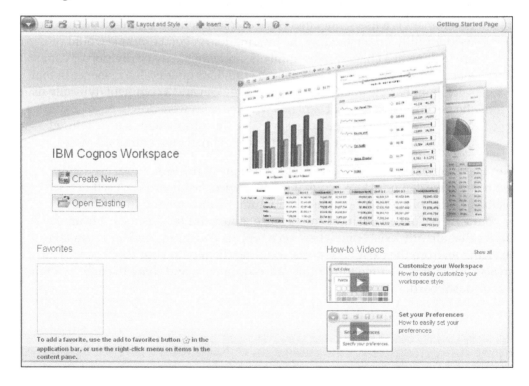

The splash screen is new to IBM Cognos Business Intelligence v10.x, but you will notice that each of the Studios now has a user-friendly welcome screen. With Cognos Workspace, you can choose from the following few options when beginning for the first time:

- **Create New**: This option will let you start with a blank canvas from which you build your dashboard
- **Open Existing**: This option will provide you with the ability to open an existing Cognos Workspace dashboard that you have access to
- **Favorites**: This section will show a sample of one of your favorite dashboards if you have added any favorites
- **How-to Videos**: This section provides videos with overviews on how to use Cognos Workspace

We will now show you how to create a new dashboard.

Adding content and content types

The first thing to consider when creating a new dashboard is what data you want to have represented. At the end of the day, a dashboard is only as valuable as the information that it provides. So the first step is to determine what data is most relevant to the business question I am trying to answer. For the purposes of this book, I will be using the sample data of IBM Cognos, and I will be creating a sales dashboard.

When you first click on **Create New**, you will see a blank canvas that will show **Drag objects from the content pane to the canvas to create a dashboard. You can also right-click an object to insert it** at the center, as shown in the following screenshot:

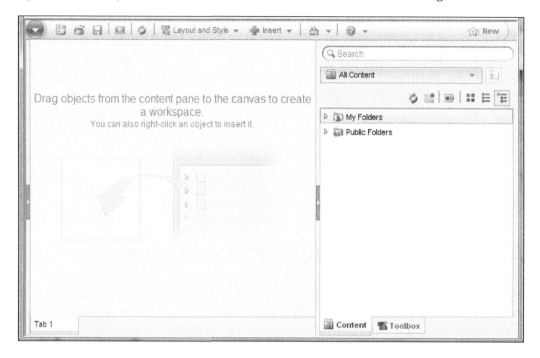

The right-hand side of this screen contains the insertable content. There are a few areas to consider. The search area will allow you to search for content that may be relevant for your dashboard. You can also navigate the content. If you choose the drop-down arrow next to **All Content**, you will have options for **My Favorites**, **My Folders**, or **All Content**. You will also be provided with a tree view of the available content in the area below the drop-down menu. To expand the tree, simply click on the folders that you would like to explore.

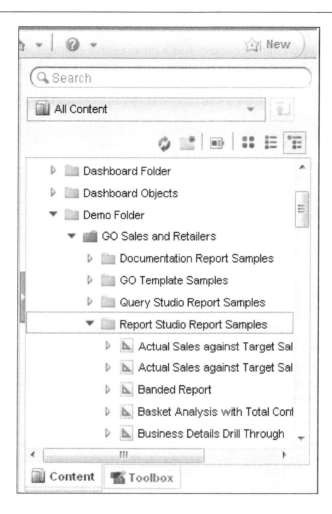

You can further expand the tree by clicking on a report. This will show you the content that is within the report. This is also where our dashboard building begins.

If you are working with reports that do not have named objects, you will simply see content that displays the type of object and a number (for example, Chart1, Chart2, List1, Crosstab1, and so on). The best practice during report development is to provide meaningful names to the objects. This is recommended so that the users of Cognos Workspace or IBM Cognos Office will have a better understanding of the content they are accessing from within the reports. The following screenshot shows an example of a naming convention in practice:

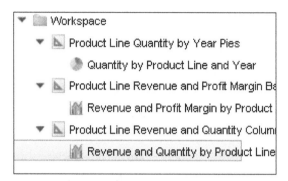

In the example shown in the previous screenshot, it is clearly seen that within the first report there is a pie chart that shows quantities for product lines and years, within the second report there is a combination chart that shows revenue and profit margin for product lines, and within the third report there is a combination chart that shows the revenue and quantity by product line.

Since I am interested in building a sales dashboard, I am going to drag each of these content objects onto my dashboard.

While dragging, the tool will provide an outline for you to gauge where you want to put the object, as shown in the following screenshot:

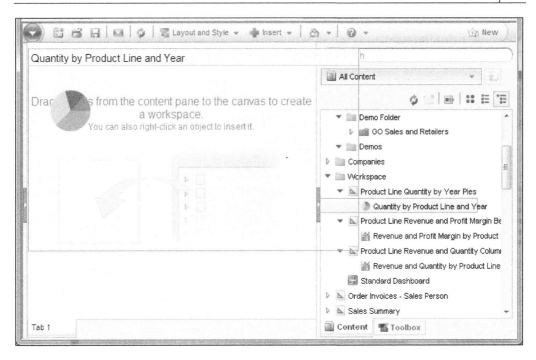

Once you drop the object, it will run the report and render the content that you are using from the report. The following screenshot is that of my dashboard after I have brought in all three of the content items from the three separate reports:

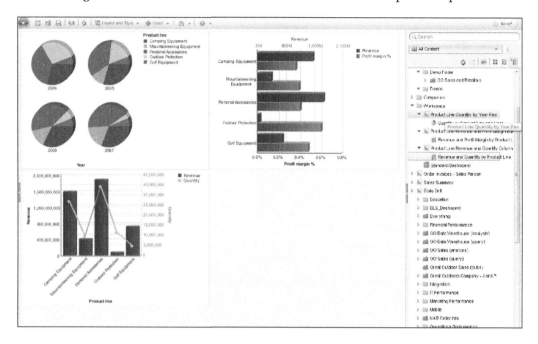

It is that simple to add basic content to a dashboard. Next, we will look at some of the things that we can do with our content now that it has been added.

Filtering

Filtering is a mechanism for limiting the data that is rendered in a report or a dashboard. A filter is going to remove the information that we do not need on our reports and only leave the information that is most relevant to us. Creating filters in Cognos Workspace is a straightforward process. The first step is to toggle from our **Content** pane to our **Toolbox**.

The Cognos Workspace toolbox contains additional objects that can be added to a dashboard besides the content. They are:

- **Web Page**: This object will allow you to embed a web page directly into your dashboard.

- **Image**: This object will add an image to your dashboard (that is, a company logo).

- **My Inbox**: This object will insert your IBM Cognos Inbox onto your dashboard so that you can manage Cognos Inbox tasks from within Cognos Workspace.

- **Text**: This object will allow you to add text to the dashboard. This is most often used for titles or instructions on the dashboard.

- **RSS Feed**: This object will allow you to add an RSS feed to the dashboard. This can be used to provide external data to your dashboard users (such as industry news).

- **Select Value Filter**: This object allows you to filter based on selected values from a list.

- **Slider Filter**: This object allows you to filter based on a slider. This filter is typically used with sequential data, such as time information or numerical data. A good example of a slider would be one that lets you say, only show me sales that were between 1 million and 5 million dollars.

On our dashboard, I am going to insert **Select Value Filter** by dragging it onto my dashboard. When I do so, a filter **Properties** window pops up.

This **Properties** window is dynamically populated based on the data available on your dashboard. For my dashboard, it is letting me choose one of my two data items to filter on (**Product line** or **Year**), and it is letting me choose which values to display in the filter. It also allows me to determine if the filter is multiselect or singleselect, the style of the filter, and the label for the filter. If I select **OK** and accept all defaults, my filter will appear on my dashboard looking like the following screenshot:

Now, if we deselect any of the product lines and hit **Apply**, we will see every chart on the page update to reflect the new filter. This is a very powerful capability for an end user, especially considering that the objects on our dashboard are all coming from different reports. This is possible because Cognos Workspace recognizes the shared dimensions by the name and common elements. For an administrator, there is no extra preparation work that is required.

Changing the formatting

Next, we will look at changing the formatting of our content. There are two common formatting changes that we can make: color schemes and chart types. Each of our charts have similar color schemes, but these might not be the color schemes that we want to use. If we hover over one of our charts, we will see the following toolbar appear above it:

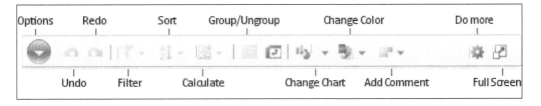

As you will notice, some of the options are grayed out for charts. These options are available when working with lists. The following are the options that you will have for working with your content:

- **Options**: This section has a list of widget actions that can be performed on your content widget. They include removing the widget, printing the widget to PDF, exporting to a number of formats, viewing different versions of the widget, refreshing the widget, reprompting the widget, resetting the widget to its original state, listening options (what filters the widget listens to), automatic resizing, moving behind other objects, doing more, and properties.

- **Undo**: This option will undo changes that you make to a list report.

- **Redo**: This option will redo changes that you have undone previously.

- **Filter**: This option will allow you to provide data filters on a list object.

- **Sort**: This option will allow you to sort your list of data by whichever column is selected at the time this option is clicked.

- **Calculate**: This option will allow you to insert new calculated columns. You would first need to select the columns on which you want to perform a calculation.

- **Group/Ungroup**: This option will allow you to group your data columns. A group will create summaries at every change in the column that is selected.

- **Change Chart**: This option will allow you to change your chart type to a different chart type.

- **Change Color**: This option will allow you to change the color scheme for the chart.

- **Add Comment**: This option only works if a report has been saved. It will allow you to add a note to a widget. This is a key component for collaborating in Cognos Business Intelligence.

- **Do more**: This option will allow you to edit the object in Cognos Workspace Advanced. This is a securable feature that will only be available to the users who can develop their own queries.

- **Full Screen**: This option will make the widget expand to a full screen.

If we select the option to change the color, we will see a complete list of all the color schemes defined, as shown in the following screenshot. These can be customized if your company has a color scheme that they would like to use for all the dashboards.

By making all of your objects share one color scheme, you can make a more standardized-looking dashboard.

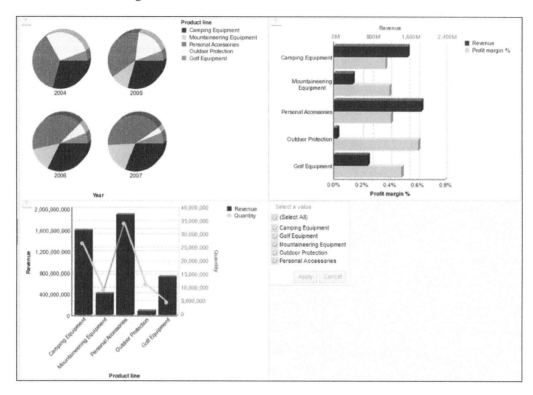

We can also change the chart type for one of our reports to better represent the data. I will change our pie chart into a line chart so that I can see more clearly how each product line has changed over time. In the drop-down box, we will select **Line Chart** as shown in the following screenshot:

Now after making many formatting changes, our final dashboard will look like the following screenshot:

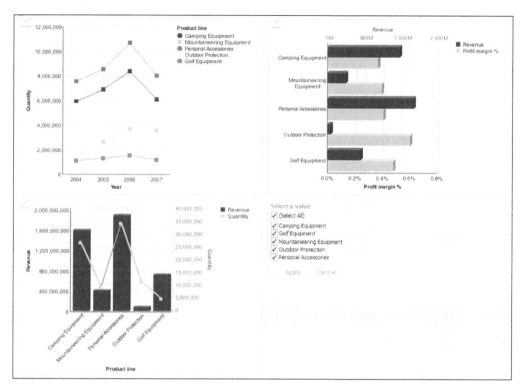

Next we will look at how we can share these dashboards with others in our organization.

Sharing the dashboard

The first and most important step for sharing a dashboard is creating it and making it fit a common business need. So far, we have looked at creating the content and customizing our dashboard. Now we can look at adding comments and saving our dashboard to a shared location for others to access it. We can finish a dashboard by saving it to a public location and adding comments to any of the objects that we think need an explanation. I will save our report and put a comment on the edited chart to explain why I changed it. This comment can contain whatever information we think is pertinent for sharing with the other users.

The comment is shown in the following screenshot:

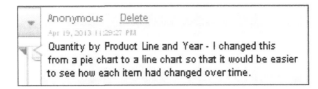

Then, when a future user opens this dashboard, they can hover over the chart and see my note. By saving the dashboard in public folders, you are able to allow others to access it and share the information that you created.

In addition to having the ability of being saved, the dashboard can be e-mailed to the other users from within Cognos Workspace by clicking on the envelope icon within Cognos Workspace.

The business case for Cognos Workspace

This section sounds like a catchy name of a webinar or a clever marketing campaign. However, there really is a strong business case for Cognos Workspace. This product was purpose-built for the business users and relies on the business users to drive the acceptance of it.

As we have discussed, Cognos Workspace is all about empowering the business user. The simplest business case for this product is the ability of someone in the business to now design and build their own dashboard without IT support. This alone is a pretty powerful capability. What I would like to do though is move beyond the business case to how you and I can drive user adoption.

The easiest way to drive user adoption is from the top down, and with Cognos Workspace it is easy to gain attention from the top. When you think of dashboards, the most common type of dashboard in businesses is the executive dashboard. What I would propose as the best way to drive user adoption through an organization is to design a dashboard for one of your key executives.

Once an executive has a meaningful, useful dashboard, he would want the people who report to him to have the same information. Then those people will want their employees to have some degree of the same information. Then so on and so forth, until you are truly touching all the levels of the organization.

However, keep in mind that the strategic benefit of Cognos Workspace is the self-service nature of it. If the IT department was tasked with building dashboards for every area of the business, it could become a maintenance nightmare. So after getting your executive involved, be prepared to have other groups within the organization designing and building their own dashboards.

Summary

Cognos Workspace is a new tool for Cognos Business Intelligence that allows the end users to develop and share their dashboards. The product is designed to make it easy for the end users to choose the data that is most important to them and to consolidate it in one location. In Cognos Workspace, you can customize the color schemes of your objects and change the chart type of your charts. You can also add comments and share the reports. Cognos Workspace makes it easy for the users to access the information on their own without having to create their own queries. In short, it is the perfect tool for power-end users that know the information they want but do not have an understanding of the underlying data.

In the next chapter, we will look at another end-user interface called IBM Cognos Active Reports for interacting with IBM Cognos Business Intelligence data.

3
IBM Cognos Active Reports

Cognos Active Report is an MHT file that can be opened in a web browser. Multiple levels of the data can be embedded within Cognos Active Reports and rendered based on how an end user interacts with the report. Cognos Active Reports are new with IBM Cognos Business Intelligence v10 and are a part of a new mobile initiative (as they can be easily viewed on an iPad).

In this chapter, we will look at IBM's new offering in IBM Cognos Business Intelligence, Cognos Active Reports. We will approach Cognos Active Reports from the perspective of an end user and dive deeper into what MHT files are and how to open them. I will show you how to interact with Cognos Active Reports, and finally, we will analyze the pros and cons of using Cognos Active Reports.

In this chapter, we will cover:

- What are MHT files
- How can MHT files be read
- Pros and cons
- The business case for Cognos Active Reports
- Interacting with Cognos Active Reports

What MHT files are

An MHT file is short for MHTML or MIME HTML. MIME is the technology that allows e-mails to contain images without having to attach the images as separate files. HTML is a standard language for the web pages. Combined, MHTML allows the combination of items that would typically be accessed via links (that is, images, audio files, embedded web pages, and so on) into a single file. This file can then be accessed without a web connection. This is extremely important for use as these files do not need to have access back to the source server in order to be opened and consumed.

How MHT files can be read

An MHT file can be opened in most browsers from your PC or laptop. Microsoft Internet Explorer has supported MHT files since Version 5.0 was released in 1999. In addition, MHT files can be opened and consumed via Firefox (with an extension), Safari, Google Chrome, Konqueror, and ACCESS NetFront.

While accessing Cognos Active Reports from within a web browser on your PC or laptop is possible, it is not the true use that Cognos Active Reports were built for. The primary intention in creating Cognos Active Reports was to provide the executives the access to Cognos BI reports from their iPads while away from the office. The Apple iPad fully supports utilization of MHT files, and are the preferred medium for consumption.

Pros and cons

Now that we understand MHT files, it is important to understand the pros and cons of using an MHT file to share information.

Pros

The advantages of using the MHT files are as follows:

- Cognos Active Reports are transportable
    - They can be e-mailed
    - They can be stored on jump drives
    - They can be saved to shared areas of a filesystem

- Cognos Active Reports are great for offline consumption
  - You can execute them while away from the office
  - Field employees can access data without an Internet connection
  - Users can work in remote locations, such as airplanes

- Cognos Active Reports work with iPads
  - Executives want this
  - iPad usage is often synonymous as ease-of-use

- Cognos Active Reports can be *flashy*
  - Flashy information is more likely to be consumed than basic information
  - The wow factor is likely to bring positive attention to your business intelligence group

Cons

The disadvantages of using the MHT files are as follows:

- Cognos Active Reports files can become very large
  - Large files will bog your e-mail servers down
  - Large files will eventually become a storage issue for IT

- Cognos Active Reports are very difficult to secure
  - Similar to PDF reports, Cognos Active Reports contain a lot of information and can be effortlessly transferred
  - This also means that information can get into the wrong hands more easily
  - BSP Mail Plus is a third-party product from BSP Software that can help as it allows e-mailed content from within Cognos BI to be encrypted

The business case for Cognos Active Reports

We have already looked at one use case for Cognos Active Reports, which is the fact that executives can access data in an interactive way while away from the office. What are the other use cases for these reports? To best understand our business uses, let's revisit the benefits of Cognos Active Reports and align those to users that are most likely to need them.

- Cognos Active Reports are transportable
    - Users that are away from the office
    - Users that do not access Cognos BI directly
    - Users that travel

- Cognos Active Reports are great for offline consumption
    - Users that fly often
    - Users that are away from a desk

- Cognos Active Reports work with iPads
    - Users that are more strategic than functional (executives)
    - Users that are on the field

- Cognos Active Reports can be flashy
    - Executives
    - External users

When looking through the benefits of Cognos Active Reports, a few user groups come to mind. The first and possibly the most important are the executives. The executives often travel and work from their iPads. The executives will also often be interested in the flashy features of new products. Finally, your executives can drive this new technology to the other areas of your business. Therefore, creation of Cognos Active Reports should begin with keeping the executives in mind. The executives can consume high-level information in Cognos Active Reports, and thanks to MHT, detailed information can be available as well with the click of a button or a tap of the finger on an iPad.

Another user group that comes to mind is any field-based sales group. Often, the sales people in the field are disconnected from the data that they need in order to be most effective at their jobs. With the advent of Cognos Active Reports, sales people in the field can bring that information with them in the form of an MHT file. Then, while on-site with a client, they can bring up that client's information even if they are not connected to your company's intranet.

The final group of users that should be addressed are other field employees. At one point in my career, I consulted an electricity company that needed to provide outage information to their field employees. Each morning, a report with outage information was e-mailed to their employees, and they would use their e-mail-ready phones to interact with it. Now, with Cognos Active Reports, that report can be consumed via a device such as an iPad, and it can be more than just a static report. In this specific example, the field employees could drill down on an outage report to see information about when it went out, which breaker it was associated with, and when it was last serviced. This additional information could then convert into less effort and higher efficiency on the job.

In general, there are countless business users that could benefit from using Cognos Active Reports. The key is to find the ones that are going to add the most value to your business by using Cognos Active Reports.

Interacting with Cognos Active Reports

Cognos Active Reports are great in theory, but how do we actually interact with them in practice? That is what this section is for. We will walk through everything from opening Cognos Active Reports to understanding the different types of interactions available within one.

Opening Cognos Active Reports

As simple as it sounds, this is not always straightforward. When I was first introduced to Cognos Active Reports, I tried double-clicking to open, and it did not work. For my computer, the default action for an MHT file was to open it in Microsoft Word. This could be the case on your machine as well.

As a result, we have a couple of options. First, we can right-click on our MHT file and choose **Open with** and then choose one of our web browsers to open the file as shown in the following screenshot:

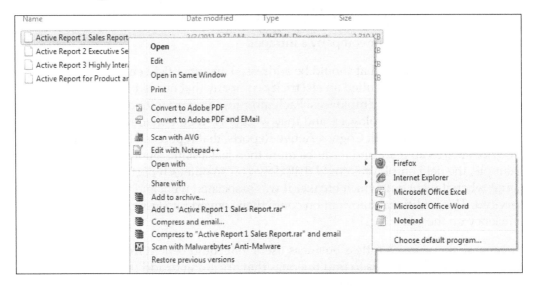

This technique will work fine if you are only opening an MHT file occasionally to consume it, but are primarily interacting with the MHT files in order to create them.

However, if your primary use of the MHT files is as a consumer, you should set a default program for opening these files and have it use one of your web browsers. This can be accomplished by right-clicking on any MHT file and choosing **Properties**. Within **Properties** of the MHT file, you will see the words **Opens with** in the middle section, and the default program for opening the MHT files.

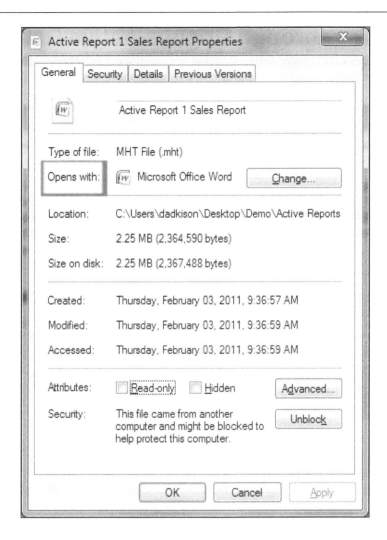

In order to set a new default, choose the button that says **Change...**, and navigate to your favorite web browser to set it as your new default program to use with MHT files.

Navigating through Cognos Active Reports

When you first open Cognos Active Reports, you will see a number of different preloaders describing what is happening in the background. The first is **Initializing Image Cache...**, which translates to loading any and all images to render on the report.

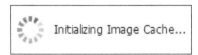

Next, you will see **Loading Application Data...**, which translates to bringing up the underlying data from the MHT file. It is worth noting that all the data loads when the report is first opened, which makes navigation within the report very fast.

Once the application data is loaded, you will see a notice **Loading Resources...**. This essentially means that all embedded information that is neither data nor images is being loaded.

After that, you will see a preloader indicating **Initializing View...**, which translates to bringing up the starting view that is defined in Cognos Active Reports.

Finally, before Cognos Active Reports renders, you will see the last preloader that states **Rendering Controls...**. This means that all the interactive components are being loaded to the page and that the HTML component of the MHTML is being displayed.

Each report will look different. Cognos Active Report is like a web page, in the sense that it can be designed to best communicate with your end users and can be navigated in any number of different ways. The following is a screenshot of a highly interactive Cognos Active Report:

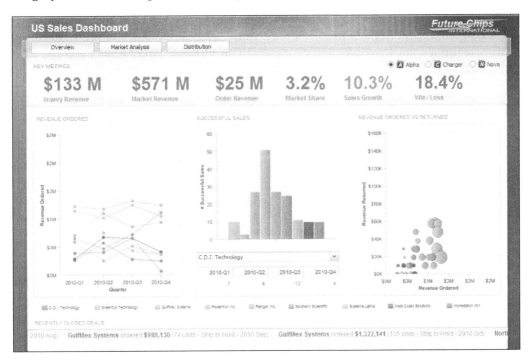

In this example, you can click on virtually any area of the report to see more information. The **Overview**, **Market Analysis**, and **Distribution** tabs each take you to separate reports. Clicking between the product groups **Alpha**, **Charger**, and **Nova** will trigger an animation that brings in the information for only the group clicked. In addition, clicking on any of the charts in the middle will update the other charts to only show the information that was clicked. Finally, the information at the bottom of the report scrolls as a scrolling marquee.

This is just one example of a Cognos Active Report. Countless examples can exist, and Cognos Active Reports can be as limitless as your imagination.

Summary

In brief, Cognos Active Reports is an MHT file that contains multiple levels of data and various types of content, all stored in a single file. There are many pros of using Cognos Active Reports to share information with your user community, the greatest perhaps being the ability to share information on the go. We looked at the various users that could benefit from using Cognos Active Reports, including but not limited to the executives, sales people, and on-the-field employees. Finally, we explored how to interact with Cognos Active Reports as an end user of the reports.

In the next chapter, we will look at interacting with Cognos BI via mobile devices. We will explore the history of mobile BI and take a deep dive into the new IBM Cognos Business Intelligence v10.2 Mobile and its support for iPad devices.

4
IBM Cognos Mobile

IBM Cognos Mobile was originally launched under the name Cognos Go! Mobile as a part of Cognos BI v8.x for delivering reports on BlackBerry, Symbian, and WinMobile phones. With the new release of IBM Cognos BI v10.1.1, the mobile offering supports immobile devices in new ways. The interface has become much more robust, and the native application for the iPad is now available in the Apple App Store. Other platforms such as those for the iPhone or Android devices are supported through a web-app-based solution. In this chapter, we will look at:

- Cognos Mobile on smartphones
- New features of Cognos Mobile
- Interacting with Cognos Active Reports on mobile devices
- The future of Cognos Mobile
- The business case for Cognos Mobile

Cognos Mobile on BlackBerry phones

Cognos Mobile has been around for about five years under the name Go! Mobile. Go! Mobile supported Windows smartphones first and then eventually also supported Symbian and BlackBerry phones. This was accomplished through an application that was installed on the device and also a server component on the Cognos BI server.

The reports that came to the phone would automatically scale for ease of use and interaction on the phone, but were far from being interactive due to the lack of a touch interface, which we see in modern phones today.

New features of IBM Cognos Mobile

With Cognos BI v10.1.1 and beyond, IBM now supports the mobile solutions in new ways. Most notably, there is now a native application for the iPad.

The advancements around the use with the iPad are all geared toward addressing a market need within the Cognos BI community. In the iPad interface, for instance, a user can now navigate their content store and have reports delivered to their device, or they can schedule reports to be delivered to their device from within Cognos BI. The big push for the use with the iPad is to use it for interacting with Cognos Active Reports and regular reports in a connected or disconnected fashion. The largest advantage is the intuitive way that the iPad is designed to be used and the way IBM has interfaced with that. You can use sliders for filtering or finger swipes for zooming or scrolling. If the report supports it, you have the ability to easily drill down into objects or drill through to other reports. Cognos Active Reports also provides an easy and compelling way to navigate your data in a disconnected fashion.

To access the new iPad application, you can download it for free from the Apple App Store. Once downloaded, locate it on your device as shown in the following screenshot:

When you open the application, you will see four sections. The first tab, **IBM Cognos Mobile**, is a welcome screen with scrolling marketing material about the Cognos Mobile application, displayed on the right-hand side of the screen. The second tab, **Reports on My iPad**, contains a list of reports that are already saved on the device. The third tab, **Get More Reports**, will allow you to connect to a Cognos BI environment via the gateway. The last one, **Get More Samples**, connects to a sample server and provides additional samples for downloading. These tabs are shown in the following screenshot:

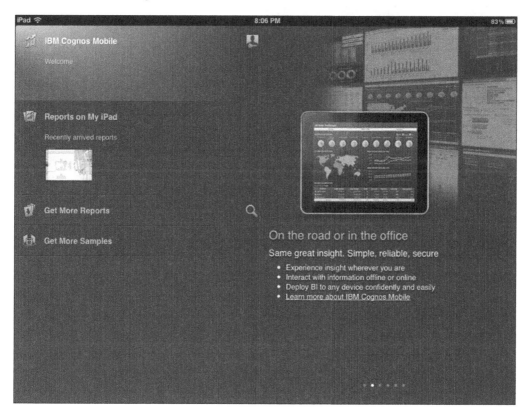

If we tap on the **Reports on My iPad** section, we will see that the application comes preloaded with one Cognos Active Report sample. More samples can be obtained by tapping on the **Get More Samples** section, as seen in the following screenshot:

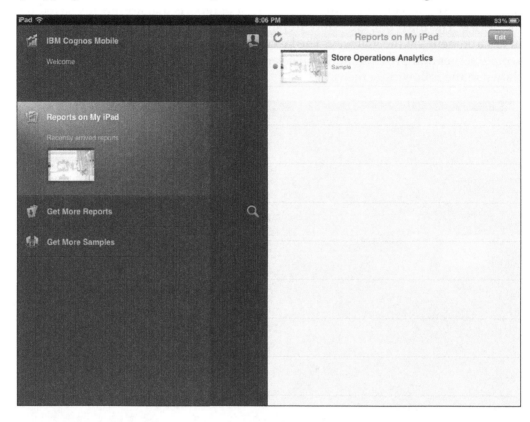

If we tap on any of the sample reports, we can see a preview of what the report looks like, with additional information about the creation date and a description of the report.

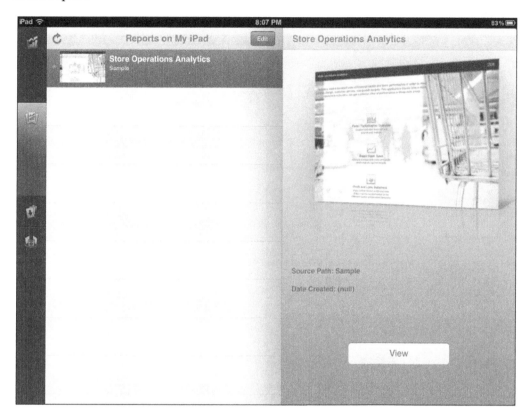

We can interact with the report once we open it.

If we tap on the **Get More Reports** section, we are prompted for a gateway and login credentials. Once logged in, we are shown **Public Folders** and/or **My Folders**, according to our access rights assigned by the administrator. We can begin navigating our content store to find additional reports.

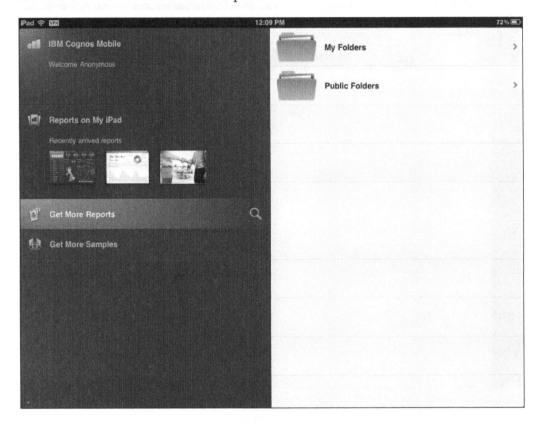

If we navigate through the folder structure, we eventually get to a level with the reports that can be run and delivered back to our device, as shown in the following screenshot:

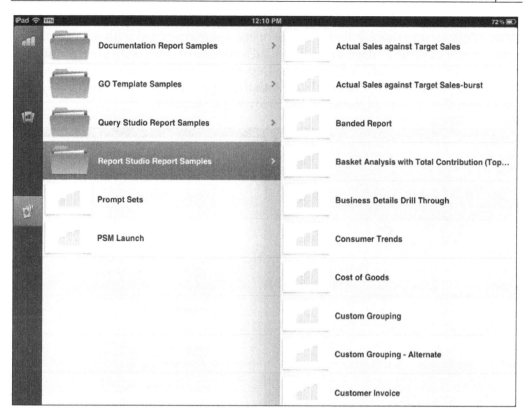

Interacting with Cognos Active Reports on mobile devices

As we discussed in *Chapter 3*, *IBM Cognos Active Reports*, Cognos Active Reports is a new way of interacting with Cognos BI content, offline. Cognos Active Reports are supported on iPad through the IBM Cognos Mobile native application. In addition, Cognos Active Reports can be opened with third-party tools such as AndReport on the Android devices.

Similar to how we interact with Cognos Active Reports in a web browser, Cognos Active Reports on a mobile device can be opened and interacted with in order to provide more detailed information. The iPad's additional touch screen capabilities make the interaction with Cognos Active Reports seem even more engaging. One great example is the **2012 Pro Football Statistics** report that is available in the **Get More Samples** section, as shown in the following screenshot:

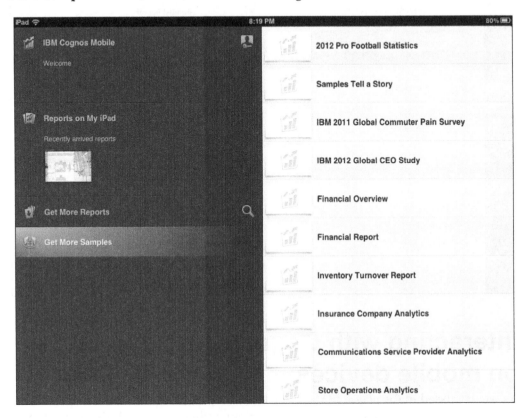

If you open this report, you are able to interact with American professional football data in a user-friendly interface.

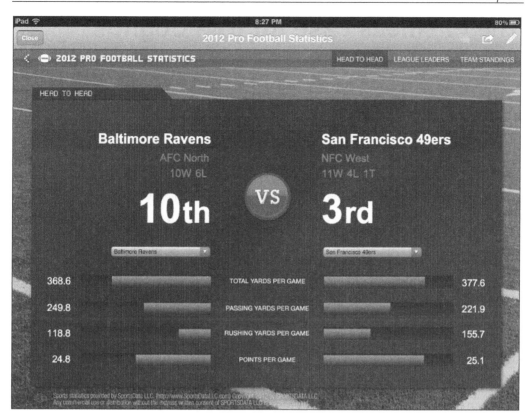

The future of IBM Cognos Mobile

In the last two years, IBM has grown their **Research and Development (R&D)** group for IBM Cognos Mobile from a small team to a larger, well-staffed team. They are now planning quarterly releases of new versions of IBM Cognos Mobile so that they can quickly release new enhancements to the market to meet their customers' increased focus on mobile devices. This additional investment in R&D is bound to mean quick advancements in the Cognos Mobile technology.

I do not feel that the goal of IBM is to replicate what competitors are doing, but rather to capitalize on their own strengths. Many people see third-party tools such as Roambi as competitors to IBM Cognos Mobile. I think that IBM will continue to allow Roambi to perform the functionality that it does well (allowing users to reauthor reports from Cognos BI data). IBM seems more focused on extending their own strengths, one of which is the ability to author once and consume anywhere.

The business case for IBM Cognos Mobile

As workforces become more mobile, so must our technology. Many businesses are replacing traditional desktop or laptop computers with iPads or other tablet devices that allow their employees to not be tied to a desk.

IBM Cognos Mobile is staying on top of this trend. When your workforce moves away from the conventional office setting to a more modern, working-on-the-go approach to business, your business analytics need to keep up. The nice thing about the recent support received from iPad is that it is flashy and can be an easy sell.

The business user that will benefit from IBM Cognos Mobile is someone who does not spend hours sitting at a desk every week. Sales people are a perfect example of a group within your organization that would benefit from a mobile solution because of its disconnected capabilities. The executives appreciate the highly visual and interactive dashboards provided by Cognos Active Reports. Imagine being able to provide your executives with Cognos Active Report, which tells them exactly how the business is doing right before they get on a plane. They can access it from their iPad during the flight, and thanks to the data and visualizations that are embedded within Cognos Active Report, they can interact with the information that you have provided them without requiring access to the BI server.

Similar to dashboards, the propagation of a mobile-reporting solution through an organization should start at the top. The executives have tablet devices and they need information. Why not provide them with the information they need on the devices that they are most likely to want to interact with it?

Summary

In summary, IBM Cognos Mobile has come a long way since its beginning as Cognos Go! Mobile, in supporting Windows Mobile phones. The product is growing, and with that growth we are seeing new ways to interact with information on the go. IBM Cognos Mobile today is an excellent tool for interacting with and running Cognos BI reports on your mobile device. The addition of Cognos Active Reports makes this offering even more valuable to an organization that is looking to enable their mobile workforce.

In the next chapter, we will look at the business-user interfaces for Cognos BI. We will start off with exploring IBM Cognos Query Studio, which is a tool designed for ad hoc reporting. Cognos Query Studio was introduced with IBM Cognos ReportNet and allows users to create basic reports very quickly. *Chapter 5, IBM Cognos Query Studio*, explores the interface and also explores how to create a basic report using Query Studio.

5
IBM Cognos Query Studio

In this chapter, we will look at Cognos Query Studio. Cognos Query Studio is a tool designed for creating ad hoc reports. Cognos Query Studio was added to the Cognos BI suite of products with the release of IBM Cognos ReportNet. The interface is designed for ease of use and provides many different drag-and-drop and right-click options for developing basic reports. In this chapter we will look at:

- Who should use Cognos Query Studio
- Accessing Cognos Query Studio
- An introduction to metadata
- The drag-and-drop interface and the right-click menu
- Saving and sharing reports
- The business case for Cognos Query Studio

Who should use Cognos Query Studio?

Cognos Query Studio is designed for the user that understands the data from which they are collecting information but will likely have a number of different, unique report requirements. The reason that this is an ideal user is because, if the user does not understand the underlying data, they are likely to be lost when trying to create their own report. In addition, if the user has only a few report requirements, they could ask IT to develop those reports for them. Therefore, with Cognos Query Studio, a business user can create their reports without having to rely on IT.

A typical user of Cognos Query Studio may be a business analyst or line-of-business user that understands their data. The understanding of the data is essential because it is very difficult to make the metadata that IT will provide simple enough for a user that does not understand what it is that they are looking at. There are ways of adding additional details to the metadata (for instance, by using the screen-tip option in Framework Manager); however, the user will still need to have at least a basic understanding of their data.

Accessing Cognos Query Studio

Accessing Cognos Query Studio is really quite simple. There are a couple of ways to do so. The first option for accessing Cognos Query Studio is from the welcome screen. On the welcome screen, you will see an option that says **Query my data**, which will launch Cognos Query Studio and allow you to select a package to build a report from.

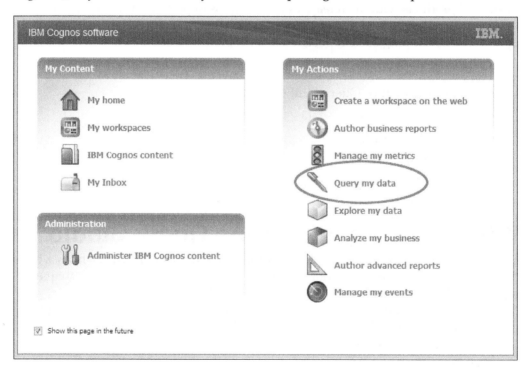

Alternatively, if you want to first navigate through **Public Folders** to the package that you are most interested in, you can choose **Query Studio** from the **Launch** menu. This is shown in the following screenshot:

Cognos Query Studio is going to open in the same browser window that you were using for navigation. This is a key feature to note as you will need to use the back navigation from Cognos Query Studio if you want to get back to Cognos Connection.

Once in Cognos Query Studio, you will see a blank area in the center where you can create your new query. Think of this blank area as your canvas and the menu on the left as your palette. In addition, you have ways of manipulating the objects that you insert by using any of the options at the top of the blank area as shown in the following screenshot:

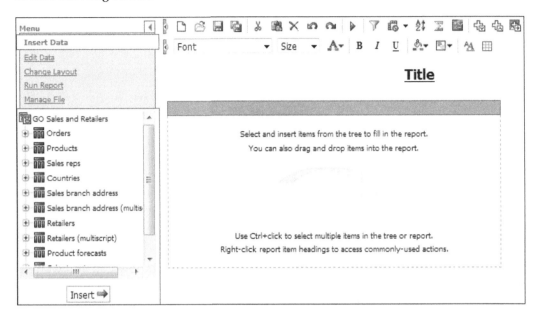

An introduction to metadata

When you first enter Cognos Query Studio, the default menu is the **Insert Data** menu. This menu will show the metadata of the package that you are in. You may be wondering what metadata is. Metadata is data that describes other data. In this case, the metadata that is displayed will be logical names for the data that is shown. This metadata is defined in Framework Manager during package design.

Look at the following example; each group of metadata (**Orders**, **Products**, **Sales reps**, and so on) is called a query subject. Within each query subject, there are a number of query items.

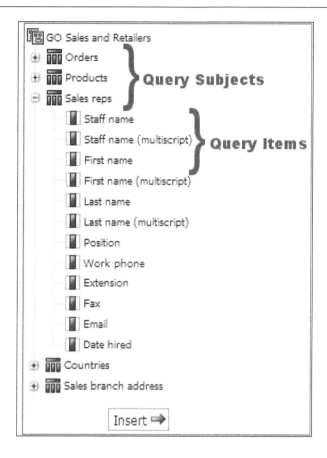

Query subjects are collections of data that are all related in some way. These collections of data can all come from one table or multiple tables. The beauty of Cognos BI is that when the query subject is presented to the end user (as seen previously), it doesn't matter where the data is coming from. On the backend, a Framework Manager modeler has taken care of all of the necessary work by designing a model to bring the data together into one view. This can be from multiple sources or a single source.

Query items are made up of information from the underlying tables that can be brought into reports as single columns of information. When we think of these query items, we often think of individual table columns from a data source. However, these facts can be made up of information from a single column or multiple columns of information brought together into one **query item through a calculation**. This again is done by a Framework Manager modeler behind the scenes.

Both query subjects and query items are often given logical, business names that do not necessarily correspond to the column names from which the data comes. We can consider a good example of this by using the example of a fact column in a table that is named `f_qty_sld`. This column is likely to represent the quantity sold for a specific item or set of items. With metadata, we can present this column to our end users as `Quantity`. In this way, we are presenting a column title that makes more sense when viewed on a report but are not changing the underlying data. In addition, we could format `Quantity` by setting the tool to automatically add a comma as the thousand separators and remove decimals. This does not have to correspond with how the data is stored in the database because Cognos BI will transform the data before presenting it to the end user based on our metadata settings.

In short, metadata allows us to present data in a more readily useable way. We are not changing the underlying data but are simply changing how it is presented to an end user.

The drag-and-drop interface and the right-click menu

Cognos Query Studio was designed with ease of use in mind. The tool uses a drag-and-drop interface and a right-click menu to accomplish most objectives of report development. In this section, we will review that interface and explore how to insert content, add filters, create calculations, format your report, incorporate charts, and understand the other buttons.

Inserting content in a report

With Cognos Query Studio, we begin with a blank canvas. The first step to designing an ad hoc report is determining what question you are attempting to answer. If you are in HR, you may want to know the average sick days per employee by office. If you are in finance, you may want to build a complete profit-and-loss statement or a balance sheet from your financial data. If you are in sales, you may want to explore sales for each branch or sales representative. Knowing what you want to present on the report is the first step to developing a good report.

Once you know what you want to build, you can start to explore your metadata to determine what content needs to be added.

Let's look at an example. In our example, we will assume that we are a sales manager for Boston and that we want to know how well our sales team is doing against their targets. The first thing that we would want to do is bring in sales representatives, branch locations, sales, and target sales (as these are the items that we are going to be reporting on).

The palette actually tells us of a few ways in which to insert these items from our metadata as can be seen in the following screenshot:

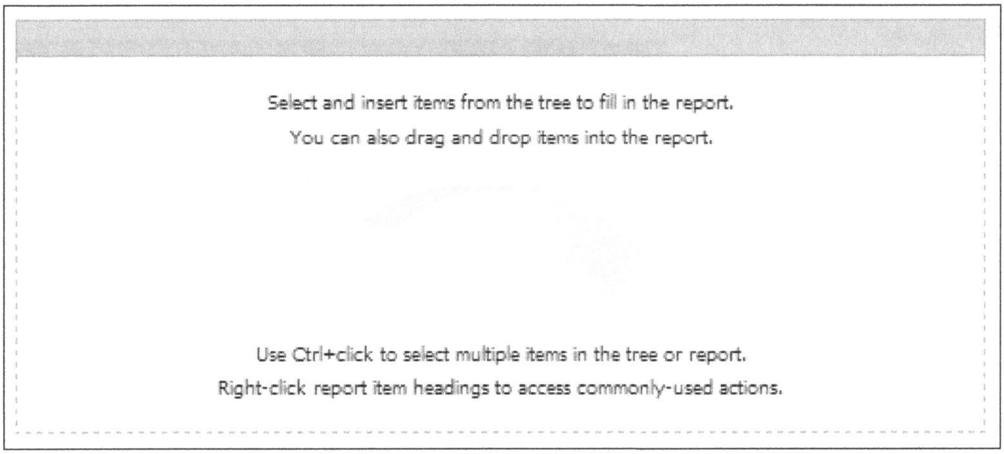

As you can see, we can drag-and-drop items onto the palette to begin creating our report. We can also double-click on an item to add it to the palette.

With our example, we want to start by adding the **First name** and **Last name** query items from the **Sales reps** query subject. We will do this by simultaneously pressing *Ctrl* and clicking on both items and dragging them to the palette as shown in the following screenshot:

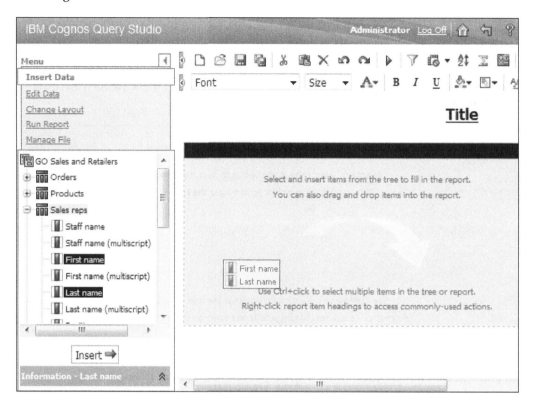

We will continue to add **City** from **Sales branch address**, **Revenue** from **Orders** and **Planned revenue** from **Orders**. When we are done, we will have a base report that looks like this:

Title

First name	Last name	City	Revenue	Planned revenue
Alessandra	Torta	Milano	$3,977,790.94	$4,145,024.42
Allisia	Wilcox	Boston	$939,511.70	$975,925.40
Ana	Orozco	Distrito Federal	$2,106,321.08	$2,267,110.32
Anders	Nilsson	Kista	$4,679,621.60	$5,027,712.56
Ashley	McCormick	Seattle	$1,979,658.62	$2,051,689.84
Audrey	Lastman	Seattle	$3,869,392.34	$4,244,344.96
Bart	Scott	Seattle	$1,561,528.96	$1,606,012.36
Belinda	Jansen-Velasquez	Amsterdam	$1,382,044.98	$1,439,380.50
Bengt	Gradin	Kista	$3,713,354.08	$3,824,063.86
Björn	Winkler	München	$9,042,091.24	$10,143,476.02
Brendon	Pike	Toronto	$2,677,171.00	$2,935,686.32
Carole	Claudel	Toronto	$3,267,821.16	$3,578,314.54
Chad	Michaels	Miami	$1,259,908.78	$1,374,172.68
Chang-ho	Kim	Seoul	$919,956.82	$1,012,384.82
Chin-Tsai	Fang	San Chung	$1,639,163.78	$1,756,923.78
Corey	Wright	Los Angeles	$640,339.14	$670,755.78
Dale	Fowler	Los Angeles	$817,514.76	$847,570.18
Daniel	Turpin	Lyon	$1,377,895.46	$1,462,576.38
Dave	Smythe	Melbourne	$1,150,116.88	$1,223,015.64
Donald	Chow	Toronto	$7,543,375.80	$8,317,229.66

≍ Top   ≗ Page up   ⬇ Page down   ≍ Bottom

Next, we want to filter this report to limit the amount of data that we are looking at to only show the group that we care about (our Boston sales team).

Adding filters

Adding a filter can be accomplished in one of two ways. The first way is by selecting the item that you want to filter on and then clicking on the filter icon in the toolbar area at the top:

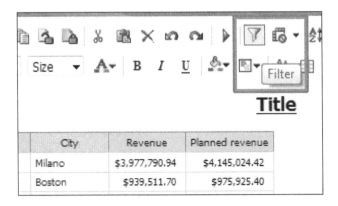

The second way to accomplish this is through your right-click menu. You can click on the column that you want to filter, right-click, and then choose **Filter...** from the right-click menu:

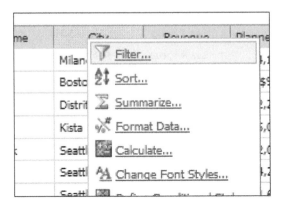

Within the filter screen, we have a few options. The first option is **Show only the following** and **Do not show the following (NOT)**. We can then choose to search for the values we want to filter by selecting **Search for values** or type in values by selecting **Type in values**. We can also choose to have the report prompt every time it runs by checking the **Prompt every time the report runs** box.

For our example, we will choose **Show only the following**, and we will choose **Boston** from the checklist and click on **OK**:

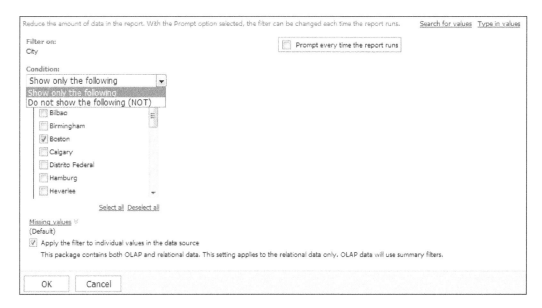

Performing this action will filter our data substantially to only show the four employees that work on our sales team out of the Boston office.

Next, we will create calculations to merge First name and Last name together and to determine how well our sales team is doing against their targets.

Creating a calculation

Creating a calculation, like most things in Cognos Query Studio, can be accomplished from both the navigation at the top and the right-click menu. To create a calculation, we can select the query items that we want in the calculation. Let's start by looking at joining First name and Last name together. To do this, we will simultaneously hit *Ctrl* and click on both of those columns. Then we can click on either the **Calculate** icon on the top or the **Calculate**... option on the right-click menu as seen in the following screenshots:

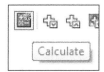

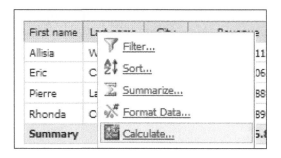

This is where things get a little interesting. The product is actually smart enough to tell the type of data that we are looking at. Therefore, for our example, we will see a set of calculations related to character-based data, that being the nature of our data.

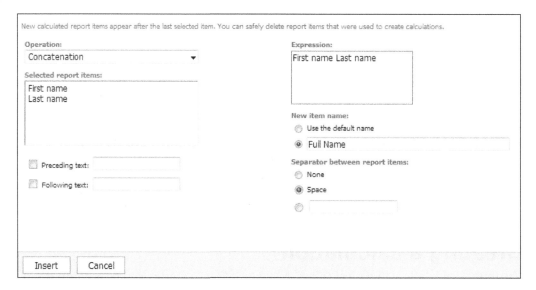

We will choose **Concatenation** as the operation that we want to perform, as seen in our previous screenshot. We will also rename our item to Full Name and select **Space** from the **Separator between report items** option.

Next, we want to look at creating a calculation on numeric columns. Since we can currently see our revenue and our planned revenue by the sales representatives, we now want to determine how close each sales representative is to their target. The way we will do that is by creating a calculation to show us each person's variance from their target.

Using the same technique discussed previously, we can select `Revenue` and `Planned Revenue` and then click on calculation icon or choose **Calculate...** from the right-click menu.

The difference is that we will now see a set of calculations based on these numeric data items:

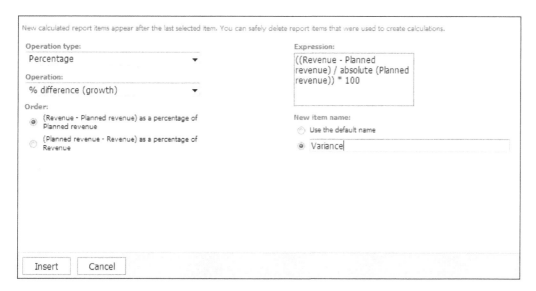

In this example, we will choose **Percentage** from the **Operation type** option and **% difference (growth)** from the **Operation** option. We will also change our new query item name to `Variance`. Once we have our options selected correctly, we will click on **Insert** to add this new calculated column.

At this point, we have all of the content that we need on our report, and we can begin looking at how we can change the formatting of this report to make it more meaningful.

Formatting your report

The first step to formatting our report in a more meaningful way is to clean up the unnecessary columns. With all of the information that we want added to our list, we now want to remove unnecessary columns by simultaneously holding down *Ctrl* and clicking on the columns no longer being used to select them. The columns that we are no longer using are `First name`, `Last name`, and `City`.

Once we have selected them, we can either hit the *Delete* key on our keyboard or click on the **Delete** icon in Cognos Query Studio.

In this scenario, because we have a filter on `City`, we will be prompted to determine whether we want to delete the filter as well. We should uncheck the filter to make sure that it is not deleted. Now your report should look like the following screenshot:

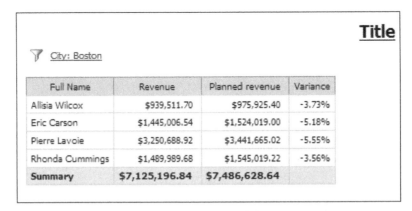

To make the information in this report stand out even more, we can add conditional formatting. Conditional formatting is formatting that is based on the data. In our example, we are going to assume that is it ok to miss your target by up to 5 percent but that anything more than that is considered poor performance. In order to invoke this conditional formatting, we will revisit our right-click menu by right-clicking on our new column, `Variance`, and clicking on **Define Conditional Styles...**:

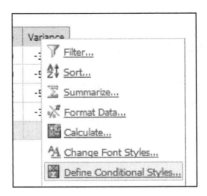

On the conditional styles menu, you can set thresholds for different formatting. In our example, we will assume that we want to be within 5 percent of our targets and will set a threshold of -.05 (or negative 5 percent) and have our number formatted with the predefined format for poor performance. The following screenshot shows an example of this:

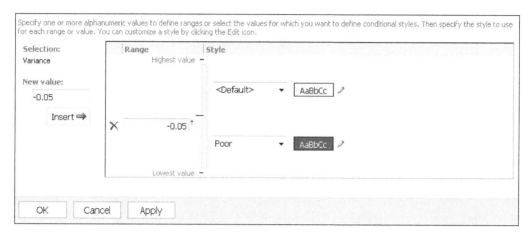

We can also change the background color and font color of our headers by highlighting all of the headers and simultaneously pressing *Shift* and clicking on Full Name and Variance. We can then click on the icons for font color.

Choose the **White** color for the font color. Next, select the paint bucket to set the background color. Here, we will choose **Navy**.

We will also click on the **bold** button to make the headers stand out more.

We can now double-click on the **Title** area to add our own custom title. We can make the title of our report `Sales Variance Report` and use a subtitle of `Boston`. Since we are using Boston in the subtitle, we can uncheck the **Show filters** option to show the filters (as well as the other options if we want) and click on **OK**:

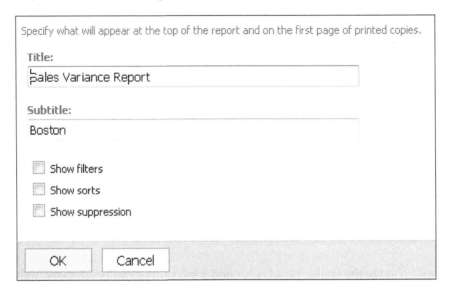

After we have completed our formatting by adding a conditional format for the `Variance` column, changing the formatting of our headers, and adding a title to the report, it should look like the following screenshot:

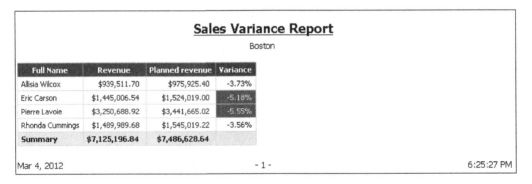

Next, we will look at enhancing this report with a chart.

Incorporating charts

Choosing the right chart type is an art. Despite popular belief, all charts are not created equal for all scenarios. For instance, with our previous example, if we were to choose a column, bar, or line chart, it would be next to impossible to see changes in our variance by the sales representative. Since variance is only a fraction of revenue and planned revenue, we have to use a chart that shows variance on a separate scale.

We can add a chart from either the **Change Layout** menu on the left of the studio or through the chart icon in the top navigation.

For this chart, we are going to use a pie chart, because it will create multiple pies and allow us to compare by measuring columns to see how each representative is performing. As you can see from the following list of chart types, there are a variety that we can choose from and a few options are available within each type. We will choose a **Standard with 3-D Visual Effect** pie chart. For other scenarios, we could also have chosen a **Column**, **Bar**, **Line**, **Column-Line** (a combination chart), **Area**, or **Radar** chart.

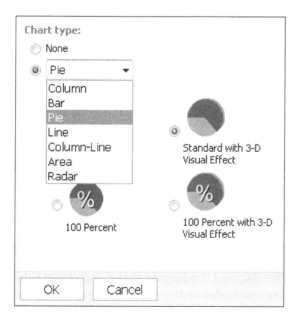

Our final report with our formatted list report and an added chart will look like the following screenshot:

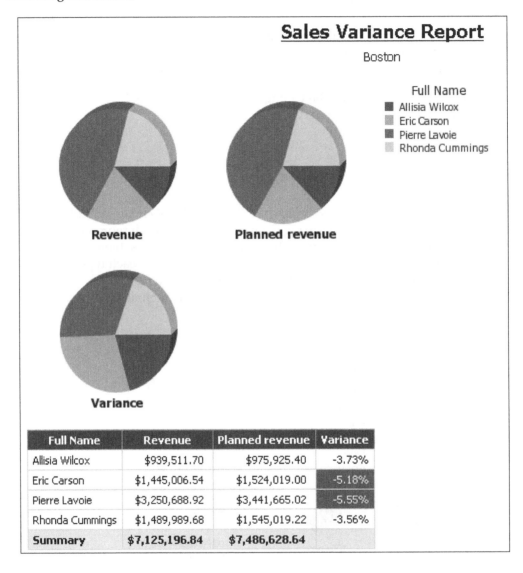

With this, we can clearly see from the chart that **Pierre** is our largest revenue generator; however, he also had the largest target and missed that target by the highest percentage than any sales representative. Next, we can look at what all of the other buttons do.

Understanding your other buttons

All of the other buttons at the top are divided into sections, and these sections correspond to menus on the left menu area. Let's walk through the buttons in each section and discuss how each button is used.

The **Edit Data** menu is what we have spent a decent amount of time in so far. This menu can be found on the left of the navigation, but the options within it are also available at the top of the screen as seen in the following screenshot:

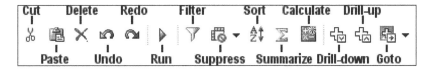

- **Cut**: This option will allow you to move an item in conjunction with the **Paste** option.

- **Paste**: This option will drop an item that you have previously cut.

- **Delete**: This option will remove the selected item from the report.

- **Undo**: This action will undo whatever last action or actions you performed.

- **Redo**: This action allows you to redo an action that you have undone.

- **Run**: This option will allow you to run the report with the data.

- **Filter**: This option will allow you to select a smaller set of data based on a specific column's data.

- **Suppress**: This option will allow you to suppress zeroes in the crosstabs.

- **Sort**: This option will allow you to sort your dataset based on a specific column.

- **Summarize**: This option will allow you to create totals, averages, and other summaries of columns of data.

- **Calculate**: This option can be used to create custom calculated fields.

- **Drill-down**: This option will allow you to navigate to the next level within hierarchical data.

- **Drill-up**: This option will allow you to navigate up a level in hierarchical data.

- **Goto**: This option will allow you to link to a separate report while passing the contents of the row of data that is highlighted as a parameter to the new report. This functionality is set up in Cognos PowerCubes or through drill-through definitions in the report.

The next section in the top navigation corresponds to the **Change Layout** menu on the left. This section allows you to customize the layout of the page. The buttons available here can be seen in the following screenshot:

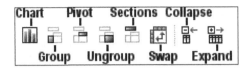

The buttons in this section are:

- **Chart**: This button allows you at add a chart to your report
- **Group**: This option will group common items in a column
- **Pivot**: This option will create a crosstab and move the selected column to the column section and leave the other columns as rows
- **Ungroup**: This option will ungroup a previously grouped column
- **Sections**: This option will create breaks at each change in data for the column selected
- **Swap**: This option will switch your rows and columns in a crosstab
- **Collapse**: This option will collapse an expanded, hierarchical data set
- **Expand**: This option will expand a hierarchical data set

The style toolbar is also located at the top of the screen. This toolbar deals with font and table formatting.

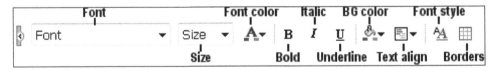

On the style toolbar, shown in the previous screenshot, we have the following options:

- **Font**: This option allows you to choose a font style
- **Size**: This option allows you to set the size of your font
- **Font color**: This option allows you to choose a color for your font
- **Bold**: This option makes the font thicker
- **Italic**: This option makes the font italic

- **Underline**: This option underlines the font
- **BG color**: This option allows you to choose a background color for your font
- **Text align**: This option allows you to select the alignment of a cell
- **Font style**: This option provides the same options as those provided by the **Font** option plus the option of a strikethrough style
- **Borders**: This option allows you to change the formatting of your table borders

We have now covered all of the formatting options for the report that are available in the toolbars. We can next look at the saving options that allow us to share our newly created report with other users.

Saving and sharing reports

Sharing reports and all other created content is done by saving the content to a location that can be accessed by the users that you want to share the data with. We will look at how we save to a public folder and how we access reports that others have created, as sharing goes both ways after all.

If we look at our final section of the toolbar, we see the four icons shown in the following screenshot:

These icons are all geared toward report creation, accessing, and saving. Here's what they do:

- **New**: This allows you to create a new report from scratch
- **Open**: This allows you to open a report that has previously been saved
- **Save**: This will save the report that you are in
- **Save as**: This allows you to save a report to a new location

Best practices would have a report developer saving a report to their **My Folders** location during development. Once a report is complete and ready for sharing, they can use the **Save as...** option and put the report into a **Public Folders** location that can be accessed by others.

The business case for Cognos Query Studio

Cognos Query Studio was designed for business users that have questions about their data but do not have time to wait for IT to create reports for them. It is designed to put the power back in the hands of the end user for creating and sharing ad hoc reports.

The simplest business case for this tool is that it is an easy-to-use option for accessing data that has not already been provided to you in an IT-built report. Many business users understand their data well enough to find the information that they need. They just need a safe, controlled means for accessing that data. While IT is often responsible for creating many production reports that are sent out to clients or are part of a reporting project, there are often scenarios where users need additional information and do not have time to wait for it. Cognos Query Studio bridges that gap between the business and IT that cannot always be filled with professionally designed reports.

The end result of providing key business users with Cognos Query Studio will be fewer report creation requests for IT and happier end users. End users want to feel enabled. If you are walking into a meeting with your boss and are the manager of the Boston branch of your company (as in our previous example), it is incredibly impressive to be able to go into Cognos BI and create a report that allows you to show exactly how each member of your team is performing. Since the business often drives the purchasing of a business intelligence tool, showing them this tool and allowing them to play with it could lead to a farther reaching Cognos BI deployment, and in turn, more success for the BI team at your organization.

Summary

Cognos Query Studio is a tool that allows end users to create ad hoc reports. No technical know-how is needed to use this tool as it is designed to be incredibly user friendly and intuitive.

In this chapter, we looked at the typical user of Cognos Query Studio. We also looked at how to access the tool and create ad hoc reports using it. We explored the various functionalities available in the toolbars, and finally, we looked at why a business would want a tool like this.

In the next chapter, we will move on from ad hoc reporting and explore the ad hoc analysis that is made available through Analysis Studio.

6
IBM Cognos Analysis Studio

Cognos Analysis Studio is a tool designed for end users that ask detailed analytical questions of their data. The tool was designed for ad hoc analyses of data by business users. In this chapter, we will cover:

- Who should use Cognos Analysis Studio?
- Accessing Cognos Analysis Studio.
- An introduction to multidimensional data.
- The drag-and-drop interface and the right-click menu.
- Saving and sharing Cognos Analysis Studio reports.
- The business case for Cognos Analysis Studio.

Who should use Cognos Analysis Studio?

Cognos Analysis Studio is intended for business users and was designed to be an easy-to-use tool for analyzing data.

A straightforward way to identify a user that would benefit from Cognos Analysis Studio is to determine what kind of questions they will ask. If they ask questions with the word *by* in them, they are likely to benefit from using Cognos Analysis Studio. For instance, a typical Cognos Analysis Studio user might ask the question, "What are our sales by year?". Another more complex question they may ask could be, "What was our margin last year by territory, by product?". These questions imply the need for examining data in a multidimensional format. That is exactly what Cognos Analysis Studio was built to do. If your business users ask questions using a combination of what, when, where, and who, it's probably an analysis.

Accessing Cognos Analysis Studio

Before we can start using Cognos Analysis Studio to analyze our data, we need to look at how to access the tool. Much like Query Studio, there are a couple of ways to access it.

The first way to access Cognos Analysis Studio is from the welcome screen by choosing the **Analyze my business** option:

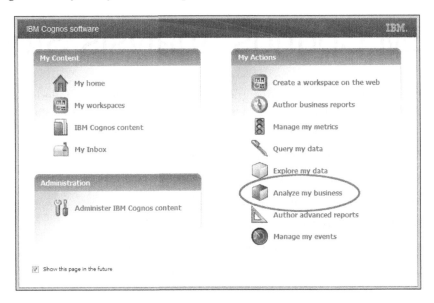

The other way to access Cognos Analysis Studio is through the **Launch** menu, choosing **Analysis Studio**:

You will then be prompted to choose a package from which you want to perform your analysis. For the sake of an example, I will use the Cognos BI sample package, **great_outdoors_8**. This is built with Cognos Great Outdoors Cognos PowerCube.

When the tool is first launched, you will be asked to start with either of the options: **Blank Analysis** or **Default Analysis**. The **default analysis** can be set up by an administrator; it is a starting analysis from which to begin creating new analysis. You can also choose whether or not to be prompted again in the future.

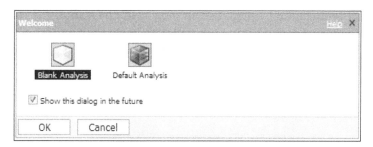

For our purposes, lets start with the **Blank Analysis** option.

An introduction to multidimensional data

When you first open the package in Cognos Analysis Studio, you will notice that the **Insertable Objects** area has a list of dimensions, hierarchies, and measures that can be added to the analysis report. The following are a couple of quick definitions for **dimension**, **hierarchy**, and **measure**:

- **Dimension**: A dimension is a grouping of data that describes other data. Dimensions contain different levels with members that roll up to one or more hierarchies. For example, a sales representative can be a dimension because you could say that a sales representative has sold a certain amount or has certain accounts roll up to them.

- **Hierarchy**: A hierarchy is the way that different dimensions roll up to one another. An easy example of a hierarchy would be time. In a time hierarchy, you can have the various days (dimensions) roll up to a month dimension. From there, the various months (dimensions) roll up to a year dimension. These rollups are levels. A level is a part of the hierarchy that allows rollup and/or drilldown. This will allow you to see the data at the previous or the next level.

- **Measure**: A measure is any numerical value (or attribute that can be counted) that an organization is interested in measuring over multiple dimensions to help run its business. A great example of a measure would be something like revenue, sales, or quantity. These are all data items that can be tracked and assigned to a dimension.

In the following example from the **great_outdoors_8** package, you can see examples of dimensions, hierarchies, and measures:

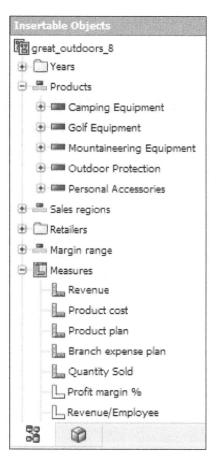

The **Products** item is an example of a dimension. **Camping Equipment**, **Golf Equipment**, **Mountaineering Equipment**, **Outdoor Protection**, and **Personal Accessories** are all examples of levels. **Revenue**, **Product cost**, **Product plan**, **Branch expense plan**, **Quantity Sold**, **Profit margin** %, and **Revenue/Employee** are all examples of measures.

Exploring the drag-and-drop interface and the right-click menu

Let's now look at actually creating an analysis by using the drag-and-drop functionality and the right-click menu. Just like we saw with Query Studio, the goal of creating Cognos Analysis Studio was to make the user interface as simple as possible. Let's explore it!

Inserting dimensions and measures

We will start by adding dimensions and measures to our analysis. If we look at the drop zones of the analysis, we can see that they clearly label where you should drag-and-drop each element with labels that say **Rows**, **Columns**, and **Measure**:

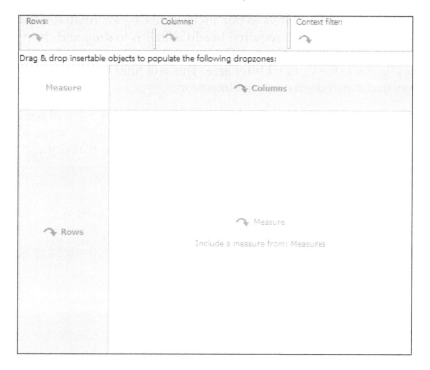

For the purpose of our example, we will drag in **Years** to **Columns**, **Products** to **Rows**, and **Revenue** to **Measure**.

Once complete, our analysis looks like the following screenshot:

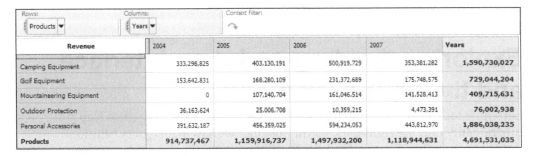

Revenue	2004	2005	2006	2007	Years
Camping Equipment	333,298,825	403,130,191	500,919,729	353,381,282	1,590,730,027
Golf Equipment	153,642,831	168,280,109	231,372,689	175,748,575	729,044,204
Mountaineering Equipment	0	107,140,704	161,046,514	141,528,413	409,715,631
Outdoor Protection	36,163,624	25,006,708	10,359,215	4,473,391	76,002,938
Personal Accessories	391,632,187	456,359,025	594,234,053	443,812,970	1,886,038,235
Products	914,737,467	1,159,916,737	1,497,932,200	1,118,944,631	4,691,531,035

The real value of this analysis is that you are able to identify cross-points for two dimensions at once. For example, we can see revenue by both **Products** and **Years** at the same time, as seen in the preceding screenshot. We will now look at filtering this data by an additional dimension.

Adding context filters

Next, we will look at adding filters to our analysis. In Cognos Analysis Studio, this is a very simple task. All that is required to add a filter is to drag-and-drop the item that you want to filter into the **Context filter** area. We will now drag in **Americas** from **Sales regions** to the **Context filter** area. This will filter the data to only show the numbers that match the **Americas** dimension.

Once the filter is in, if we click on the down arrow to the right, we will see a list of the levels within **Americas** and hover over each of the countries to see a list of cities and then each city to see a list of sales representatives in that city.

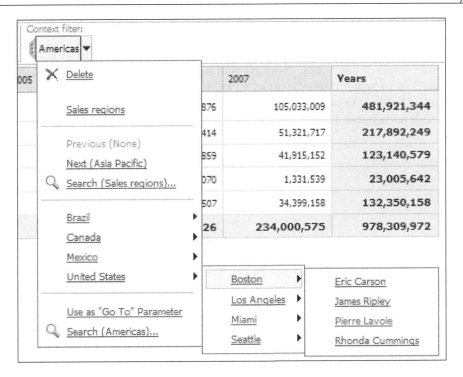

With this context filter in, we can also choose to change the filter to a different region or add additional filters in order to further limit the data.

We also have the option of bringing in additional filters and continuing to limit our data.

The filter option is often used when you are trying to answer a question with the word *for* in it. For example, if I wanted to know our company's revenue by year for **Americas**, that is an example of the analysis from the previous example. In addition, if you wanted to know sales revenue by **Year** for **Americas** and for a **Margin range** dimension set between 0 and 20 percent, we could continue to limit the data by dragging in the **Margin range** dimension as another filter.

Drilling down and expanding data

One of the key capabilities of Cognos Analysis Studio is the ability to navigate through the different levels of your data. Working within our existing data, I am going to drill down into 2006 in order to see the quarters below 2006 and the data associated with each quarter. In order to perform this drill-down mechanism, we either click on **2006** or right-click and choose **Drill Down** from the right-click menu:

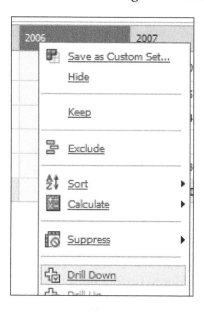

This is an excellent feature if you want to drill down on one dimension. However, what do you do if you are interested in drilling down on all levels? With Cognos Analysis Studio, we have a couple of options. Let's look at these for our other hierarchy, **Products**.

If I right-click on the thin bar above my list of products on my rows, I can see a complete menu of capabilities including the ability to expand or drill down a level on all of the items at once:

One neat thing to note is that the right-click menu is customized to the dimension you are clicking on. In this case, it says that we can expand products. When we choose the **Expand Products** option, we will see the next level beneath the items that are part of the base level under the **Products** dimension.

This next level is going to show up nested to the right of the starting level:

Revenue		2006 Q 1
Camping Equipment	Cooking Gear	5,242,575
	Lanterns	2,777,196
	Packs	8,284,693
	Sleeping Bags	7,474,212
	Tents	10,997,494
	Camping Equipment	**34,776,170**
Golf Equipment	Golf Accessories	1,349,768
	Irons	5,815,865
	Putters	2,191,119
	Woods	7,709,572
	Golf Equipment	**17,066,324**
Mountaineering Equipment	Climbing Accessories	1,863,207
	Rope	3,160,740
	Safety	2,304,978
	Tools	3,831,582
	Mountaineering Equipment	**11,160,507**
Outdoor Protection	First Aid	112,260
	Insect Repellents	396,967
	Sunscreen	230,410
	Outdoor Protection	**739,637**

Nesting is a useful way to see another level of information without losing the level that we started with. Nesting is taking one level from the same or a different dimension and placing it beneath or alongside your original level. It is a very powerful tool in the arsenal of a Cognos Analysis Studio user.

Another option for seeing the next layer of detail in a hierarchy is the **Down a Level** option:

This other drill option on the right-click menu will allow us to go down a level without keeping the original level. This is useful when you want to see a complete list from that level without necessarily needing to know how each parent item rolls up in the hierarchy. A great example of using this would be if you wanted to see a complete list of your product names without the parent levels being displayed. Conveniently enough, the lowest level in our **Products** dimension has a list of products. Therefore, if we choose the **Down a Level** option twice in a row, we should see a complete list of our products as rows in our analysis.

What we notice, however, is that our list is truncated with the **More** option to show more and to keep as much information as possible on the screen for analysis:

Revenue
TrailChef Canteen
TrailChef Cook Set
TrailChef Cup
TrailChef Deluxe Cook Set
TrailChef Double Flame
TrailChef Kettle
TrailChef Kitchen Kit
TrailChef Single Flame
TrailChef Utensils
TrailChef Water Bag
EverGlow Butane
EverGlow Double
More
Total

If we click the **More** option, we are prompted for how many items we would like to display in the rows so that we can bring in the entire list.

The final option that we will look at for expanding our data analysis is the ability to nest levels from different dimensions. We mentioned a moment ago that nesting items which are not alike can help us to better understand our data and is often one of the best friends of a Cognos Analysis Studio user. Let's look at how nesting works. Nesting is the action of inserting a level inside or below another level. It is accomplished through drag-and-drop and is very simple to do. We will first nest a level inside our **Products** dimension. If you are following along, we have used the **Up a Level** option to bring the view back up to the first level within the **Products** hierarchy:

We have also deleted the filter on **Americas** from the **Context filter** area.

What we can do now is drag-and-drop our **Sales regions** dimension onto our palette along with our **Products** dimension. During this drag-and-drop, you will notice that there are a few different places that you can drop the dimension, and each will perform a different task. Also, Cognos Analysis Studio gives you different visual cues about where you are about to drop the new dimension. This is called nesting nodes.

Replacing the existing dimension

To replace the existing dimension, drag the new dimension on top of it. You will know that you are in the correct spot because the existing dimension will be highlighted in black as shown in the following screenshot:

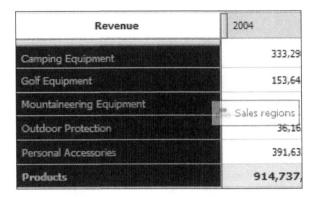

Revenue	2004
Camping Equipment	333,29
Golf Equipment	153,64
Mountaineering Equipment	Sales regions
Outdoor Protection	36,16
Personal Accessories	391,63
Products	914,737

Once you release the mouse, you will see the new dimension appear where the original dimension was as seen in the following screenshot:

Revenue	2004	2005
Americas	192,342,219	
Asia Pacific	166,861,815	
Central Europe	428,893,362	
Northern Europe	70,278,517	
Southern Europe	56,361,554	
Sales regions	914,737,467	

Nesting within the existing dimension

To nest within the existing dimension, drag the new dimension slightly to the right of the existing one. You will know that you are in the correct spot when you see a black line with a white box around it showing up to the right of your existing node as seen in the following screenshot:

Revenue	2004	2
g Equipment	333,298,825	
uipment	153,642,831	
ineering Equipment	0	
r Protection	Sales regions	
l Accessories	391,632,187	
ts	**914,737,467**	

Doing this will nest the new dimension inside the existing one so that you can see within each product line how much revenue there was for each sales region. This is a very useful tool for answering the more complex questions where the word *by* is used multiple times. The end result will be a very robust analysis as seen in the following screenshot:

Revenue		2004	2005
Camping Equipment	Americas	104,350,317	122,537,142
	Asia Pacific	87,851,472	107,499,821
	Central Europe	71,690,887	89,503,966
	Northern Europe	39,224,688	45,810,361
	Southern Europe	30,181,461	37,778,901
	Sales regions	**333,298,825**	**403,130,191**
Golf Equipment	Americas	48,288,489	49,259,629
	Asia Pacific	42,407,234	44,704,380
	Central Europe	32,318,598	36,612,013
	Northern Europe	16,497,530	19,711,020
	Southern Europe	14,130,980	17,993,067
	Sales regions	**153,642,831**	**168,280,109**
Mountaineering Equipment	Americas	0	32,065,568
	Asia Pacific	0	29,890,443
	Central Europe	0	22,616,016
	Northern Europe	0	11,879,335
	Southern Europe	0	10,689,342
	Sales regions	**0**	**107,140,704**
Outdoor Protection	Americas	11,319,521	7,188,512
	Asia Pacific	9,437,031	6,460,387
	Central Europe	8,120,363	6,175,966
	Northern Europe	3,906,862	2,727,239

Nesting below an existing dimension

To nest a new dimension below an existing dimension, drag the new dimension slightly below the existing one. For this example, you will know that you are in the correct spot when you see a black line with a white box around it showing up below your existing row dimension as seen in the following screenshot:

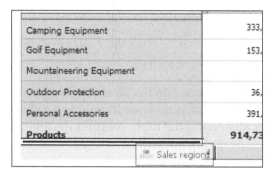

This mechanism for nesting dimensions allows you to answer questions that have the word *by* in them as well as the word *and*. For instance, if you were asked, "What are our **Revenue** numbers by **Year**, by **Product** and **Sales region**?", you could answer that question with the analysis we just created, which is known as a discontinuous crosstab and is shown here:

Revenue	2004	2005	2006	2007	Years
Camping Equipment	333,298,825	403,130,191	500,919,729	353,381,282	1,590,730,027
Golf Equipment	153,642,831	168,280,109	231,372,689	175,748,575	729,044,204
Mountaineering Equipment	0	107,140,704	161,046,514	141,528,413	409,715,631
Outdoor Protection	36,163,624	25,006,708	10,359,215	4,473,391	76,002,938
Personal Accessories	391,632,187	456,359,025	594,234,053	443,812,970	1,886,038,235
Products	914,737,467	1,159,916,737	1,497,932,200	1,118,944,631	4,691,531,035
Americas	192,342,219	239,401,452	312,565,726	234,000,575	978,309,972
Asia Pacific	166,861,815	212,448,438	276,319,000	205,165,272	860,794,525
Central Europe	428,893,362	539,441,359	676,044,507	500,200,108	2,144,579,336
Northern Europe	70,278,517	90,294,795	117,379,677	92,104,996	370,057,985
Southern Europe	56,361,554	78,330,693	115,623,290	87,473,680	337,789,217
Sales regions	914,737,467	1,159,916,737	1,497,932,200	1,118,944,631	4,691,531,035

While this looks like a very simple report, it actually contains a wealth of information and would allow us to answer a variety of questions from one screen.

With all of these options, how do we know what to nest where and when to use a specific type of nesting? It still comes back to the question you are asking. Here is a bit of a guide:

- If you are asked to show information based on an existing analysis, but with a different dimension being used, you can drag-and-drop to replace a dimension

- When you are asked to provide an analysis that shows many different dimensions (or many **bys** in the question), use the "nest within" option

- On the occasions that you want to have a filter that is not part of the crosstab, you can use the context filter to limit your analysis

Finally, when you are asking a question that uses *by* as well as *and* (for instance **Revenue** by **Year**, by **Product** and **Sales region**), you can use the "nest beneath" or "nest beside" option.

Creating calculations

Let's now look at expanding the analysis that we have with calculations. We have made it pretty clear that using Cognos Analysis Studio is all about answering questions. So, what do we do when we are asked a question and we don't have the data already available to us in the package we are exploring? We essentially have two options. We can either ask the people in our organization that manage our package creation to update PowerCube, OLAP data source, or dimensionally-modeled relational data source to include the data we need, or we can try to create it from the data that is available to us. Why don't we try an example?

We will assume that we have been asked to provide information on what our average revenue was from 2004 to 2007 by product and region. If we start with our analysis that has **Revenue** for **Products** by **Years** and **Sales region**, all we need to do in order to answer this question is create a calculation to show the average for the entire year and then clean up the formatting a bit.

To create a calculation on the four years 2004 to 2007, start by selecting all of them. This can be accomplished by pressing *Ctrl* and clicking on each or by simultaneously pressing *Shift* and clicking on the first and last items (**2004** and **2007** respectively).

Once all items are selected, you can right-click to see your right-click menu and then hover over **Calculate** to see a list of your calculation options:

Revenue	2004	2005	2006	2007	Years	
Camping Equipment	333,298,825	403,130,191	500,919,729			0,027
Golf Equipment	153,642,831	168,280,109	231,372,689			4,204
Mountaineering Equipment	0	107,140,704	161,046,514			5,631
Outdoor Protection	36,163,624	25,006,708	10,359,215			2,938
Personal Accessories	391,632,187	456,359,025	594,234,053			8,235
Products	914,737,467	1,159,916,737				1,035
Americas	192,342,219	239,401,452				9,972
Asia Pacific	166,861,815	212,448,438				4,525
Central Europe	428,893,362	539,441,359				9,336
Northern Europe	70,278,517	90,294,795	117,379,677			7,985
Southern Europe	56,361,554	78,330,693	115,623,290	87,473,680	337,789,217	
Sales regions	914,737,467	1,159,916,737	1,497,932,200	1,118,944,631	4,691,531,035	

Menu overlay:
- Save as Custom Set...
- Hide
- Keep
- Exclude
- Sum (2004, 2005, 2006, 2007)
- Average (2004, 2005, 2006, 2007)
- Minimum (2004, 2005, 2006, 2007)
- Maximum (2004, 2005, 2006, 2007)
- Custom...
- Calculate ▶
- Go To ▶
- Show Attributes ▶
- Properties (Years)

You will notice immediately that, like our other right-click menus, our calculation options are automatically showing options based on the data type that we have selected and dynamically populating a few popular options for that data type with the dimensions selected. For our purposes, our calculation is available on this menu. However, if it were not, we could choose the **Custom...** option to see a complete list of calculations or to build out a more complex calculation. For this scenario, let's go ahead and select **Average (2004, 2005, 2006, 2007)**, and in doing so, we will see a new column created that shows the average for those four years.

Next, for the sake of cleaning up the report, we will once again highlight **2004**, **2005**, **2006**, and **2007**, as well as **Years** and right-click again to hide these columns using the **Hide** option. In doing this, we replace all five of those columns with a single column that says, **More & hidden**. We can actually right-click on it as well and choose **Hide** once again to remove it:

Revenue	Average (2004, 2005, 2006, 2007)	More &		
			Hide	
Camping Equipment	397,682,507		Unhide	▶
Golf Equipment	182,261,051			
Mountaineering Equipment	102,428,908		Number of Visible Items	▶
Outdoor Protection	19,000,734		Sort	
Personal Accessories	471,509,559			
Products	**1,172,882,759**		Calculate	▶
Americas	244,577,493		Properties (Years)	
Asia Pacific	215,198,631			
Central Europe	536,144,834			
Northern Europe	92,514,496			
Southern Europe	84,447,304			
Sales regions	**1,172,882,759**			

We now have the information that we need. The last thing that we will do, for
purely cosmetic reasons, is right-click on **Average (2004, 2005, 2006, 2007)** and
choose **Rename...** so that we have an easier-to-read column title:

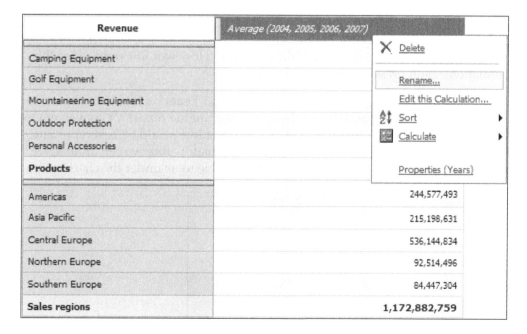

I will rename the column to `Average - 2004 to 2007`, and with that, we have created our first Cognos Analysis Studio calculation and in turn answered a question that we could not answer from the data that was already available to us. Now let's look at making this crosstab a little prettier.

Incorporating charts

A great way to jazz up any report is by adding charts. Within Cognos Analysis Studio, we have a variety of chart types available to us. The hardest part of adding a chart is always determining what chart type to use. The action of adding a chart is actually quite simple.

Choosing a chart type

Choosing a chart type can be as simple as reading it from a requirements document or as complex as needing to understand the data visualization principles that govern what charts to use and when. If you are not familiar with data visualization, it essentially covers the entire spectrum of how data is presented in a meaningful way. In a modern context, data visualization tends to refer to the presentation of data in some format of charting, and more specifically, to the different schools of thought around how to determine the best physical representation for different types of data.

To simplify this process, ask yourself the question, "How would I want to see this information?", and present it in that manner.

With the example that we used previously, if we add **Years** back to the columns to the left of **Average – 2004 to 2007**, we have a pretty unique report for conversion to a chart. So, we have to ask ourselves how this information would be best represented to provide the most information in the simplest format. Before we can do that, we should take a look at the chart types that are available to us under the chart button:

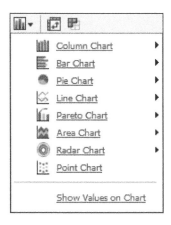

The chart types available are:

- **Column Chart**: A column chart is great for presenting various dimensions of data across time or for comparing dimensions side by side.

- **Bar Chart**: A bar chart is similar to a column chart; however, you typically see it used for dimensions other than the time dimension. Since time is thought of as linear, it is harder to picture it moving upward as opposed to from left to right.

- **Pie Chart**: A pie chart represents data as sections of a pie. This is an excellent charting type to show how various dimensions make up different portions of the whole.

- **Line Chart**: A line chart is great for showing changes over time. A line chart can be used to compare how data changes over time in the same way that a column chart is used.

- **Pareto Chart**: A Pareto chart is a way of showing data over time as well as a running total at the same time. You typically see Pareto charts used when you want to represent incremental time (like quarters) and still show a running total for those increments.

- **Area Chart**: An area chart is typically used to represent volumes. You can think of this as a combination of a line chart (where you can clearly see fluctuations across dimensions) and a bar chart (where you see the filled-in area below the data points).

- **Radar Chart**: A radar chart (also sometimes called a web chart) is a way of seeing one or more measure points depicted inside of a chart that looks like a radar. You can easily see how far objects are from the center point. You typically see this used when the center point is the goal. For instance, if you wanted to depict defects in your products on a chart, this would be a good option, because you could see which products are the furthest from the goal of zero.

- **Point Chart**: A point chart is like a line chart; however, it does not have the lines connecting the dots between the data points. You typically see this chart type used when the data is not meant to be viewed in a linear format. You see this used most often in conjunction with two equally important measures where the higher you are on the measures, the better. That way, when you see data points that are far to the upper-right, you know that those items are doing well. Conversely, items that are in the far lower-left quadrant are performing poorly. You often see these charts divided into four quadrants in order to acknowledge the fact that being strong in only one of the measures (and in turn being in the upper-left or lower-right quadrants) can still be acceptable.

With most of these charts, you also have the option of creating them as **Stacked** or **100% Stacked** charts.

- **Stacked**: A stacked chart is a chart that has measure for multiple items within a dimension placed together in one graphical item. For instance, a stacked bar chart would have multiple divisions for each bar to depict what amount of that bar was made up of each item. The following example shows a stacked bar chart:

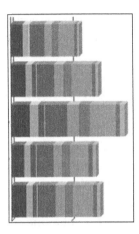

- **100% Stacked**: A 100 percent stacked chart is very similar to a stacked chart, with only one exception; in a 100 percent stacked chart, each section represents the percentage of the whole as opposed to the exact value. Therefore, all columns, bars, lines, and so on will add up to 100 percent on the chart as seen in the following example:

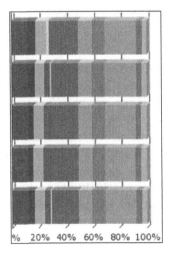

After some review, it is clear that some of these options would simply not work with the data that we have. Because we have two separate groupings adding up to the total, it is very difficult to determine what the best way to represent it might be. In reality, the best way to determine what chart will share the most in the simplest format is through trial and error. In our example, (after a bit of trial and error) you should be able to see that the best way to show the information that we have is through a stacked column chart. Since a business person would most likely care about changes over time as well as what percentage of the whole each area makes up, this is the best solution for showing these two completely separate things. In addition, thanks to the hover feature that is natively available on charts in Cognos Analysis Studio, the details for any specific section is available as well.

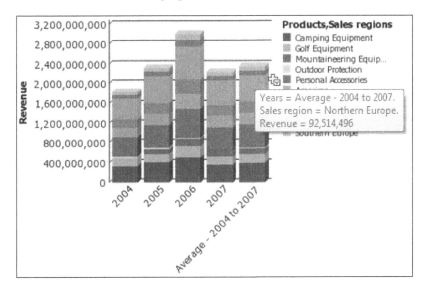

Understanding the other buttons

Now that we have reviewed how to build an analysis, learned the ways of creating calculations, and explored the world of charting, let's see what our other buttons do.

The buttons are as follows:

- **New**: This button will allow you to create a new analysis from scratch.

- **Open**: This button will allow you to open an existing Cognos Analysis Studio report.

- **Save**: This button will allow you to save your Cognos Analysis Studio report.

- **Save as**: This button will allow you to save your Cognos Analysis Studio report with a different name or to a different location.

- **Delete**: This item will delete the object or objects that are selected when it is clicked. Note that not all objects can be deleted (for instance, if you have a calculation built off an object, you will have to hide it rather than delete it).

- **Undo**: This object will reverse the last action that was performed.

- **Redo**: This button will redo the last action that was undone.

- **Search**: This button will allow you to search for a data item within a hierarchy.

- **Run**: This button will allow you to run the report. It also has a drop-down menu available for running different file outputs.

- **Go To**: This button works in conjunction with drill-throughs that have been created in the OLAP data source or with drill-through definitions. These drills-throughs allow you to link from the cube to a different report. If they exist, you will be able to find them in the **Related Links...** list when you choose this option.

- **Filter**: This button will allow you to create a filter on the items that are selected when it is clicked. You can also choose this option to remove a filter that already exists.

- **Top/Bottom**: This button will allow you to limit your dataset to only show the top X or bottom X items within a dimension based on the measure that is being used. This is very useful when you have large sets of data but want to only show the high or low performers.

- **Suppress**: This button will allow you to hide zeros or blanks based on zeros in either rows or columns.

- **Sort**: This button will allow you to sort a column or row based on the data from highest to lowest or lowest to highest.

- **Subtotal**: This button will allow you to add subtotals at breaks in your data.

- **Total**: This button will allow you to create custom totals at the end of each of your dimensions.

- **Calculate**: This button will allow you to create a calculation based on the columns or rows selected.

- **Display**: This button will allow you to change what is displayed between the crosstab, chart, or crosstab and chart.

- **Chart**: This button will allow you to select a chart type to add to the report based on the analysis that has been created.

- **Swap**: This button will switch your rows and your columns on your crosstab.

- **Custom Set**: This button will allow you to save a grouping of dimensions as a custom set of dimensions for future use with other Cognos Analysis Studio reports.

Saving and sharing Cognos Analysis Studio reports

Now that we have fully explored how to create Cognos Analysis Studio reports, we need to understand how we can share these with other individuals within our organization. In the last section, we reviewed the buttons that are used to save reports. In order to share a report, you will need to save it to a place that the person or people you want to share with can access it. To do this, first click on the **Save As** button:

You are then prompted at the bottom to choose a location to save to and a name for your new report. Be sure to save to a place in which the other users that need the report can access it.

You have just shared your newly created report!

The business case for Cognos Analysis Studio

Now that we have covered all of the technical stuff, it makes sense to examine why a business would want this functionality. The major reason to want Cognos Analysis Studio in your business is that the ability to analyze your data in a self-service, easy-to-use manner will in turn make your business more agile and your decisions more rapid. How does Cognos Analysis Studio do that? As questions arise that require a multidimensional view of data in order for them to be answered, Cognos Analysis Studio gives business users the ability to answer those questions without having to involve IT. By having an interface that allows business users that need information to access that data instantly, those business questions that come up can be answered more quickly, and the decisions that need to be made based on that information can be made more rapidly.

Think of a scenario where a client manager receives a call from the client requesting support. Perhaps during that call, the client manager needs to clearly understand what the profitability is of this client across different areas of the business and across time. Without Cognos Analysis Studio, this is information that the client manager may never have. With Cognos Analysis Studio and a well-designed data source, the client manager could bring up Cognos Analysis Studio to build a report of profitability by department, by years, for this specific client. They can then use of that information to make decisions based on past experiences.

Summary

We have looked at Cognos Analysis Studio in this chapter, focusing first on who should use the product and how they can access it. We then took a deeper dive into understanding how to use the tool while exploring everything from simple drag-and-drop analysis creation to the data visualization concepts of charting. We wrapped up the chapter by looking at why a business would want a tool like Cognos Analysis Studio.

In the next chapter, we will explore the newest business user reporting and analysis interface, Business Insight Advanced. In Cognos Workspace Advanced, we will be able to create ad hoc reports and analyses with a simple-to-use, yet very powerful interface.

7
IBM Cognos Workspace Advanced

Cognos Workspace Advanced is changing the game for business-level users in IBM Cognos BI. The product is designed to allow querying and analysis from a single interface. It interacts with and enhances Cognos Workspace and is part of the shared workspace concept within IBM Cognos Business Intelligence v10.x. In this chapter, we will look at:

- Who should use Cognos Workspace Advanced?
- Comparing Cognos Workspace Advanced to Cognos Query Studio and Cognos Analysis Studio.
- Accessing Cognos Workspace Advanced.
- Exploring the drag-and-drop interface and the right-click menu
- Using external data.
- The business case for Cognos Workspace Advanced.

Who should use Cognos Workspace Advanced?

In the last two chapters, we have looked at Cognos Query Studio and Cognos Analysis Studio. We discussed how Cognos Query Studio is designed for business users who want to create ad hoc reports. We also discussed how Cognos Analysis Studio is designed for business users who want to perform ad hoc analyses. Cognos Workspace Advanced is designed for business users that want to do both.

With Cognos Workspace Advanced, business users have one tool for creating advanced analyses and reports. The tool, like Query Studio and Analysis Studio, is designed for ease of use and is built on the same platform as the other report development tools in Cognos. Business Insight Advanced/Cognos Workspace Advanced is actually so powerful that it is being positioned more as a light Cognos Report Studio than as a powerful Cognos Query Studio and Cognos Analysis Studio.

Comparing to Cognos Query Studio and Cognos Analysis Studio

With so many options for business users, how do we know which tool to use? The best approach for making this decision is to consider the similarities and differences between the options available. In order to help us do so, we can use the following table:

Feature	Query Studio	Analysis Studio	Cognos Workspace Advanced
Ad hoc reporting	X		X
Ad hoc analysis		X	X
Basic charting	X	X	X
Advanced charting			X
Basic filtering	X	X	X
Advanced filtering			X
Basic calculations	X	X	X
Advanced calculations			X
Properties pane			X
External data			X
Freeform design			X

As you can see from the table, all three products have basic charting, basic filtering, and basic calculation features. Also, we can see that Cognos Query Studio and Cognos Workspace Advanced both have ad hoc reporting capabilities, while Cognos Analysis Studio and Cognos Workspace Advanced both have ad hoc analysis capabilities. In addition to those shared capabilities, Cognos Workspace Advanced also has advanced charting, filtering, and calculation features.

Cognos Workspace Advanced also has a limited properties pane (similar to what you would see in Cognos Report Studio). Furthermore, Cognos Workspace Advanced allows end users to bring in external data from a flat file and merge it with the data from Cognos Connection. Finally, Cognos Workspace Advanced has free-form design capabilities. In other words, you are not limited in where you can add charts or crosstabs in the way that Cognos Query Studio and Cognos Analysis Studio limit you to the standard templates.

The simple conclusion after performing this comparison is that you should always use Cognos Workspace Advanced. While that will be true for some users, it is not true for all. With the additional capabilities come additional complexities. For your most basic business users, you may want to keep them using Cognos Query Studio or Cognos Analysis Studio for their ad hoc reporting and ad hoc analysis simply because they are easier tools to understand and use. However, for those business users with basic technical acumen, Cognos Workspace Advanced is clearly the superior option.

Accessing Cognos Workspace Advanced

I would assume now that, after reviewing the capabilities Cognos Workspace Advanced brings to the table, you are anxious to start using it. We will start off by looking at how to access the product.

The first way to access **Cognos Workspace Advanced** is through the welcome page. On the welcome page, you can get to Cognos Workspace Advanced by clicking on the option **Author business reports**:

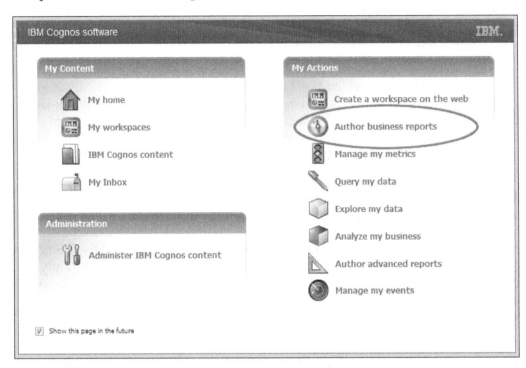

This will bring you to a screen where you can select your package. In Cognos Query Studio or Cognos Analysis Studio, you will only be able to select non-dimensional and dimensional packages based on the tool you are using. With Cognos Workspace Advanced, because the tool can use both dimensional and non-dimensional packages, you will be prompted with packages for both.

The next way to access Cognos Workspace Advanced is through the **Launch** menu in Cognos Connection. Within the menu, you can simply choose **Cognos Workspace Advanced** to be taken to the same options for choosing a package.

 Note, however, that if you have already navigated into a package, it will automatically launch Cognos Workspace Advanced using the very same package.

The third way to access Cognos Workspace Advanced is by far the most functional way. You can actually access Cognos Workspace Advanced from within Cognos Workspace by clicking on the **Do More...** option on a component of the dashboard:

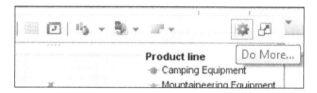

When you select this option, the object will expand out and open for editing inside Cognos Workspace Advanced.

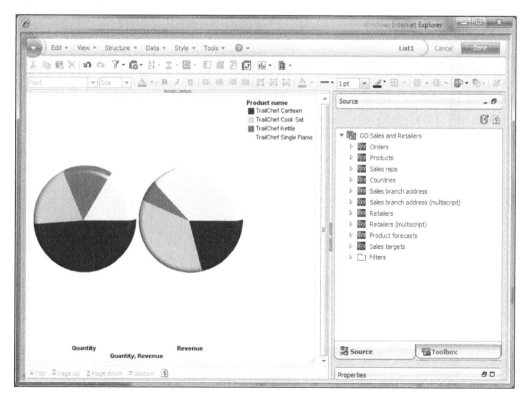

Then, once you are done editing, you can simply choose the **Done** button in the upper right-hand corner to return to Cognos Workspace with your newly updated object.

For the sake of showing as many features as possible in this chapter, we will launch Cognos Workspace Advanced from the welcome page or from the **Launch** menu and select a package that has an OLAP data source. For the purpose of following along, we will be using the Cognos BI sample package **great_outdoors_8** (or Great Outdoors).

When we first access it, we are prompted to choose a package. For these examples, we will choose **great_outdoors_8**:

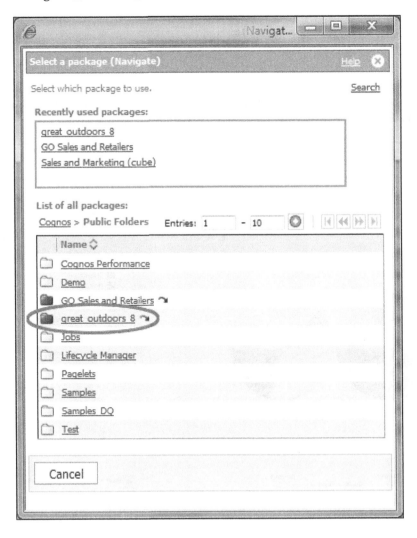

We are then brought to a splash screen where we can choose **Create new** or **Open existing**. We will choose **Create new**.

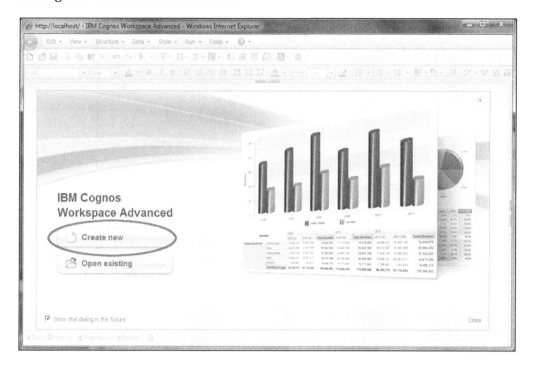

We are then prompted to pick the type of chart we want to create. As we will see from the following screenshot, our options are:

- **Blank**: It starts us off with a completely blank slate
- **List**: It starts us off with a list report
- **Crosstab**: It starts us off with a crosstab
- **Chart**: It starts us off with a chart and loads the chart wizard
- **Financial**: It starts us off with a crosstab formatted like a financial report

- **Existing...**: It allows us to open an existing report

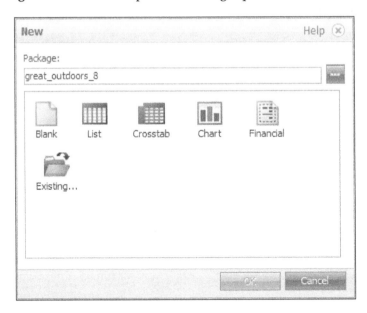

We will choose **Blank** because we can still add as many of the other objects as we want to later on.

Exploring the drag-and-drop interface and the right-click menu

Now that we have a blank template to start with, let's explore how to build a complex report and analysis using the drag-and-drop interface. With Cognos Report Studio, there is a concept of objects that can be brought onto your palette. Here, we will explore how to add these objects by clicking, holding, and moving them to the location that we want to place them in.

Adding objects to your report

The tool has a few main components. Each is listed and shown in the subsequent screenshot.

- **Toolbars**: These toolbars provide additional options for controlling your report.

- **Palette**: This is what will show up on your report. By default, the palette will load with data.

- **Insertable Objects**: These are the objects that can be added to your report.

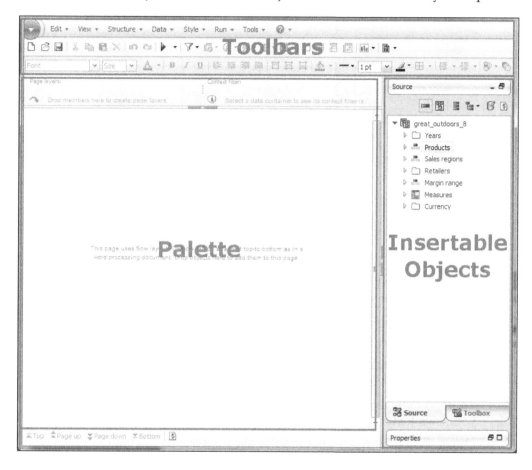

We should start by looking at the objects that we can add to our report. The **Insertable Objects** pane has two main tabs, **Source** and **Toolbox**. Source is the package that you are working on, and toolbox is a list of objects that can be added to the palette.

We will start off by building our report from the **Toolbox** area. Here we can see the list of insertable objects as seen in the following screenshot:

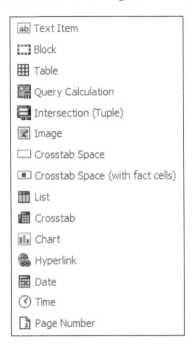

- **Text Item**: A tool with which you can define the text that is used.
- **Block**: This object is used for spacing and controlling where items appear on the report. A block is an area where other items can be inserted.
- **Table**: A table can be used to separate items in the report or for inserting your own text.
- **Query Calculation**: This item can be used to create a calculation based on data after it is aggregated in the query.
- **Intersection (Tuple)**: This allows you to add a single point of data based on dimensions and measures that you add through a wizard.
- **Image**: This allows you to add an image to your report.
- **Crosstab Space**: This option will add a blank row or column into an existing crosstab.
- **Crosstab Space (with fact cells)**: This option will add a column or row into an existing crosstab with fact cells to allow you to add additional information.

- **List**: This option will insert a list data holder for adding levels, properties, or measures (similar to what you see when using Cognos Query Studio).

- **Crosstab**: This option will insert a crosstab data holder for adding dimensions and measures (similar to what you see when using Analysis Studio).

- **Chart**: This will allow you to add one of the new chart types to the report. Data will still need to be added to it, but this gives you a wizard for selecting the chart type that you want.

- **Hyperlink**: This will allow you to create a link to another location on the Web or within your internal environment. You often see these used to link to a common area on your intranet.

- **Date**: This will allow you to add a dynamic date to the report. Each time the report is run, it will be updated with the current system date.

- **Time**: This will allow you to add a dynamic time to the report. Each time the report is run, it will be updated with the current system time.

- **Page Number**: This will allow you to add a page number to your report. If you have multiple pages, they will be automatically updated with the correct page numbers.

For the purpose of this book, we will start by adding a table to the palette and choosing two columns and two rows. We will also check the **Maximize width** option to maximize the width so that the table takes up the entire screen:

We will now proceed to add additional objects into each quadrant of our table. In the upper-left quadrant, we will add a chart. This will give us our first look at the new charts that are available for inserting. To do this, drag-and-drop a chart object into the upper-left quadrant of the table. You will then be prompted to choose what chart type to insert:

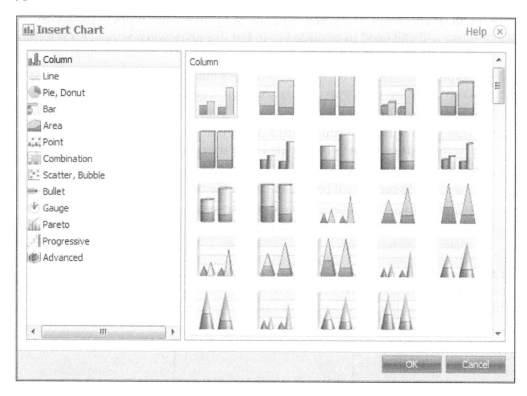

The options that are available within the **Insert Chart** window are:

- **Column**: This option allows you to choose between various column chart options, including standard column charts, cylinder column charts, and cone column charts

- **Line**: This option allows you to choose between various clustered line charts

- **Pie, Donut**: This option allows you to choose between various pie and donut chart options

- **Bar**: This option allows you to choose between various bar chart options, including standard bar charts, cylinder bar charts, and cone bar charts

- **Area**: This option allows you to choose a chart that is similar to a line chart; however, the area under the line is filled in

- **Point**: This option allows you to create charts with data points only (no connecting lines)

- **Combination**: This option allows you to create charts that have columns and lines

- **Scatter, Bubble**: This option allows you to create reports with points that are dynamic in size based on a second measure

- **Bullet**: This option allows you to create charts that reflect a measure compared to a target

- **Gauge**: This option allows you to create various forms of gauge charts

- **Pareto**: This option allows you to create Pareto charts for tracking individual data points and running totals

- **Progressive**: This option is a column or bar chart and a running total as well

- **Advanced**: This option contains 3D charts, radar charts, and heat map charts

For our purposes, we are going to start off by adding **Clustered Cylinder with 3-D Effects** from within the **Column** chart options to the upper-left quadrant. We will then drag in a second chart to the upper right-hand quadrant. For this chart, we will choose a **Horizontal Bullet** chart.

Let's continue by dragging a **List** to the lower-left quadrant and a **Crosstab** to the lower right-hand quadrant. When we are done dragging in our objects, our palette should look like:

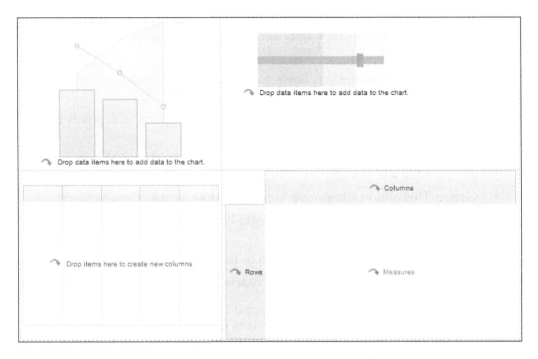

At this point, we have all of the objects that we want in our report. We need to start adding the data that we need to make this report meaningful.

Adding data to your reports

In order to add data to the report, we need to toggle back to the **Source** tab in the **Insertable Objects** area. When we do so, we will see a member tree for the package that we are working with by default. This is because the package is built from a multidimensional source; however, we could have used a relational source as well.

We can choose to change between views using the options at the top. These options are:

- **View Members Tree**: This option will show the metadata as members that can be added for multidimensional analysis

- **View Metadata Tree**: This option will show you the metadata and properties that can be added to the objects meant for reporting

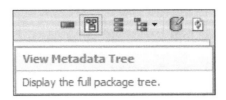

- **Create Sets for Members (currently inserting individual members)**: This option will allow you to toggle between inserting sets and individual members from a members tree

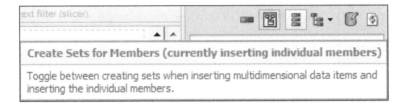

- **Insert Single Member / Insert Children / Insert Member with Children**: This option allows you to choose what parts of an object to insert when inserting a member

For our purposes, let's start by inserting members to the areas where we want to perform analysis. We will use members for the cylinder chart and the crosstab. We can begin by clicking on the cylinder chart (in the upper left-hand corner) in order to see our available drop points.

Here we have drop areas for **Categories (x-axis)**, **Default measure (y-axis)**, and **Series (primary axis)**:

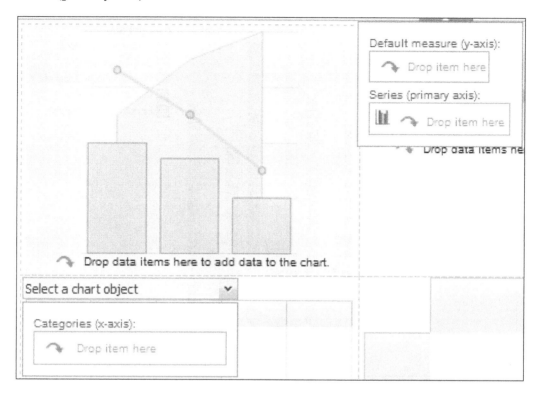

We will drag in the **Years** dimension from **Years | Years** to **Categories (x-axis)**. We will also drag in the **Products** dimension from **Products | Products** to **Series (primary axis)**. Finally, we will drag in **Revenue** from **Measures | Revenue** to **Default measure (y-axis)**. Note that once we drag in our measure, the chart is populated with data.

Our final chart in the upper left-hand quadrant should look like the following screenshot:

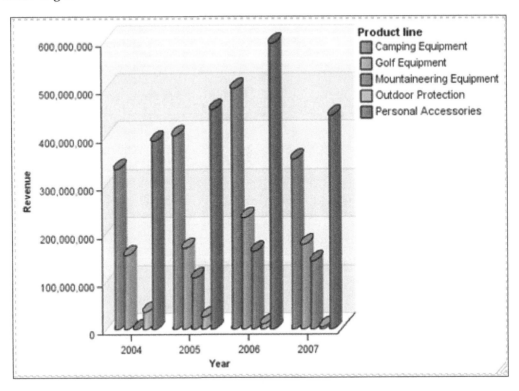

We can now begin populating our crosstab. We want to depict the same information in our crosstab. Therefore, we will drag in **Years** from **Years | Years** to **Columns**, **Products** from **Products | Products** to **Rows**, and **Revenue** from **Measures | Revenue** to **Measures**. The end result in our lower left-hand quadrant will look like:

Revenue	2004	2005	2006	2007
Camping Equipment	333,298,825	403,130,191	500,919,729	353,381,282
Golf Equipment	153,642,831	168,280,109	231,372,689	175,748,575
Mountaineering Equipment	0	107,140,704	161,046,514	141,528,413
Outdoor Protection	36,163,624	25,006,708	10,359,215	4,473,391
Personal Accessories	391,632,187	456,359,025	594,234,053	443,812,970

Now, we will toggle over to **View Metadata Tree** so that we can build our reporting objects:

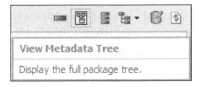

We will start by adding data to the bullet chart. If we select the bullet chart, we can see what data can be added:

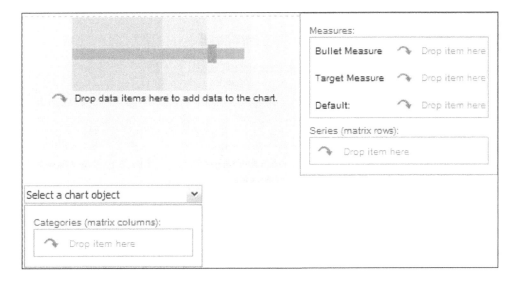

The options available are as follows:

- **Bullet Measure**: This is the measure that we are tracking and are interested in.
- **Target Measure**: This is a measure that represents what our goal is for the bullet measure.
- **Default**: This is the default measure.
- **Series (matrix rows)**: This represents rows of bullet charts that can be shown. This will do the same thing as **Categories** until there are items dropped into both areas.
- **Categories (matrix columns)**: This represents columns of data that can be shown. This will do the same thing as **Series** until there are items dropped into both areas.

We are going to drag in **Revenue** from **Measures | Revenue** to **Bullet Measure** and **Sales target** from **Measures | Sales target** to **Target Measure**. When we are done with this, we will see data. To finalize our view, we drag in **Product line** from **Products | Products | Product line** to **Categories (matrix columns)**. Our end result for the chart in the upper right-hand quadrant will look like:

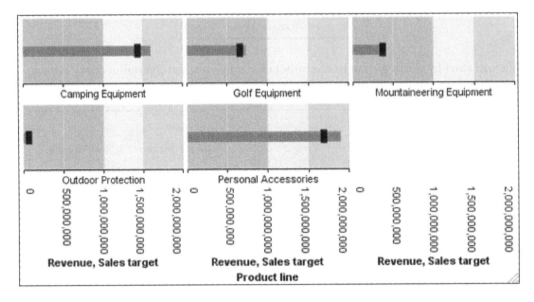

Finally, we will build out our list report by dragging in **Product line, Revenue,** and **Sales target** as columns in the lower left-hand quadrant. Our list will look like this with the new items added:

Product line	Revenue	Sales target
Camping Equipment	1,590,730,027	$1,428,960,225
Golf Equipment	729,044,204	$656,796,136
Mountaineering Equipment	409,715,631	$368,931,775
Outdoor Protection	76,002,938	$67,879,753
Personal Accessories	1,886,038,235	$1,682,800,650
Overall - Summary	4,691,531,035	$4,205,368,540

We have now added to our report the data that we want to report on and analyze.

Drilling down

The key feature needed in order to perform an analysis is a drill down. Luckily, the hard work is done on the backend during the creation of the multidimensional data source. All we have to do is let the tool know that it is ok to allow drilling. This is accomplished from the **Data** menu under **Drill Options....**:

We are given two basic drilling options from this menu. We can choose **Allow drill-up and drill-down**, which we will be sure to check now for our reporting purposes. We can also choose **Allow this report to be a package-based drill-through source**. This means that, if there are drill-throughs defined in the package, we can access them.

With our drill-down enabled, let's go ahead and run the report for the first time by choosing the blue play button at the top:

Our end result will look like:

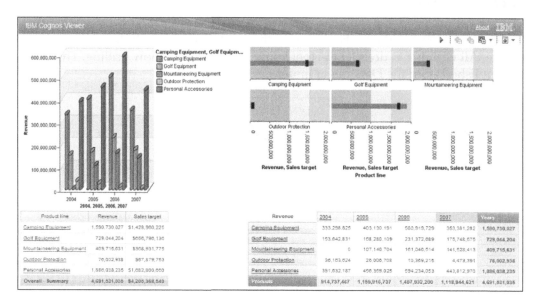

This now looks like a report. However, because we have drill-up and drill-down enabled, we can click on any component of the report and drill to the next level of detail. We can also right-click to be taken to a menu that allows us to choose **Drill Down**, **Drill Up**, or **Go To** (drill through):

As you can see, this menu also allows us to **download the chart** (saves the chart as an image), read the **glossary** (provides definitions for some items), or view **lineage** (traces the item selected back to the source).

Creating calculations

We can now begin further enhancing our report and analysis with calculations. We are going to start off by adding a calculation to our list report that is in the lower left-hand quadrant.

1. First, we will highlight **Revenue** and **Sales target**.

2. Then, we will right-click to bring up our right-click menu and choose **Calculate** and then **Custom**. From there, we can choose % **Difference** from the drop-down list.

3. We can then choose % **Difference (Sales target, Revenue)**. This will essentially give us a variance calculation.

We can choose to provide a different name for the default name as well. We will go ahead and name this one Variance. Once that is complete, you will see in the following screenshot, that it automatically formats the new column as a percentage:

Variance
11.32%
11.00%
11.05%
11.97%
12.08%
11.56%

In order to create a more complex calculation, you have to right-click on your new calculated query item and choose **Edit Query Expression...** from the list of available options. From this menu, you can freeform most calculations that Cognos BI supports.

In addition, the **Functions** tab will provide common functions, and each will show a tip if you click on it:

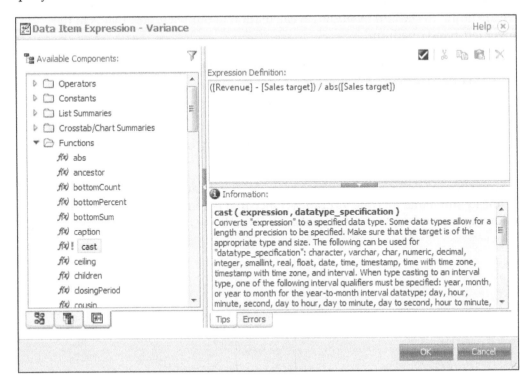

This is sort of a trick for getting the most out of Cognos Workspace Advanced. The default calculation menu will show only basic calculations; however, you are able to create more advanced calculations by editing the query in this way.

Understanding the other buttons

Now that we have covered the basics, it is important to understand our other options on the toolbar. Let's go from left to right. The first few buttons are all geared toward saving, opening, cutting, copying, pasting, and report-wide undo and redo functionality.

The buttons in the previous screenshot are:

- **New**: This option will allow you to create a new report.
- **Open**: This option will allow you to open an existing report.
- **Save**: This option will allow you to save the report for future use or to be shared.
- **Cut**: This option allows you to copy an item and move it to another place. It also erases the item from the original location.
- **Copy**: This option allows you copy an item and create a duplicate for it in a new location.
- **Paste**: This option is used to finalize the copy or cut actions with the creation of the new version of the item that was copied or cut.
- **Delete**: This option will remove an item that is selected.
- **Undo**: This option will reverse an action that was done.
- **Redo**: This option will redo an action that was undone.

The next option is to run with different run options:

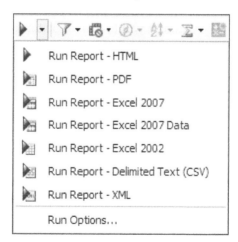

The next section has all the standard options that we have seen in the other two business-user studios:

The options are listed as follows:

- **Filter**: This option will allow you to create a filter that limits the data being retrieved
- **Suppress**: This option will allow you to remove rows or columns with zeros
- **Explore**: This option allows you to perform analysis actions on your data
- **Sort**: This option allows you to choose sorting options for your data
- **Summarize**: This option will allow you to create summary aggregations for your various measures
- **Calculate**: This option will allow you to create a calculation on any of your items
- **Group**: This option will allow you to bundle within a data item
- **Pivot**: This option will allow you to toggle from a list to a crosstab
- **Section**: This option will allow you to create sections based on the contents of a data item or dimension
- **Swap**: This option will allow you to swap columns and rows on a crosstab
- **Chart**: This option will allow you to create a chart on your report
- **Layout**: This option will allow you to choose a standard layout template for your report

In addition to these toolbars, there is a wealth of capabilities available in the menu bar and the formatting bar that can be explored for further enhancing your Cognos Workspace Advanced reports and analyses.

Using external data

Another way to expand the capabilities of this product is to bring in external data. External data is data that is not already included in the Cognos BI package that is being used. External data is typically some form of flat file (such as a CSV file). The ability to incorporate external data is a new feature in IBM Cognos Business Intelligence v10.x that is available only in Cognos Workspace Advanced and Cognos Report Studio.

In order to incorporate external data into your report, you will need to select the icon in the **Insertable Objects** area that represents the external data option.

Once you click on the icon, you will be prompted with the **External Data** wizard:

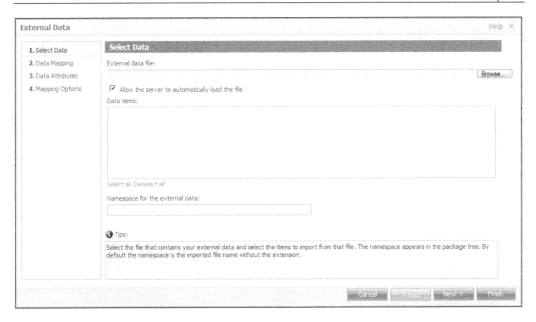

This wizard will walk you through the process of creating a connection between data that is outside of Cognos BI and data that is within a package. The first step is to select the data that you want to bring in. This is done very simply by clicking on the **Browse...** button and finding the file with the information that you want to bring in:

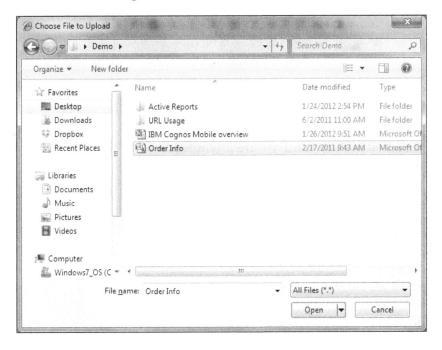

You can then choose which columns from the file to bring in and what to name the new namespace that you are adding.

After you click on **Next>**, you will be able to choose how to perform your data mapping.

You can choose an existing report (this is typically the report that you are working on; however, that is not required) to map to the external data.

For our purposes, we will choose **Product Revenue** from the **Go Sales and Retailers** folder. Here we will create a new link between the external data and the existing report by clicking on the **New Link** button. We will then click on **Next>** again:

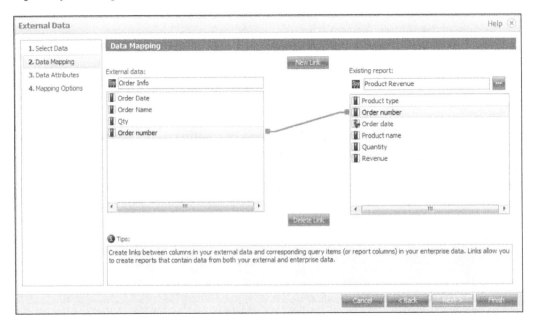

In the next section of the wizard, we are prompted to select the data attributes for the data that we have. This is possibly the most important part of this entire process.

Unfortunately, if we select the wrong data type for an item that is being linked to while on this screen, it can affect our ability to create the relationship, and we will get errors when trying to pull data from both locations at once. Once we have all the data type options set correctly, we can click on **Next>** and move on to the final step:

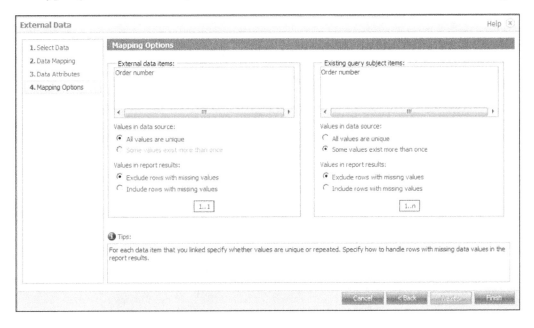

In the final step, we can choose the cardinality that we want for the relationship that ties in our external data. When we are done, we can click on **Finish**, and it will take us to a place where we can name our new package and publish it to a location of our choice:

We have now officially created a new package with external data.

The business case for Cognos Workspace Advanced

Cognos Workspace Advanced was designed for business users that want it all. So, if you have users that need both query creation capabilities and analysis capabilities, this is the tool for them. Cognos Workspace Advanced adds a tool that provides flashy graphics and an easy-to-use interface to make these tasks easier than ever before. This tool also gives the IT group the ability to better enable their business users to do the things that they have historically done for them. For the world of business intelligence, this tool changes the game for those users.

As an IT group, the best way to convince the business of the value of this tool is to simply show it to them and then allow them to use it. As they find themselves more empowered to create their own reports and develop their own analysis, they will realize that this product decreases the time from question to answer for your business users.

Summary

Business Cognos Workspace Advanced adds the ability to perform queries and create analyses from one central location. It also further enhances the new Cognos Workspace product by allowing users to take an object from Cognos Workspace and further enhance it within this development product. In this chapter, we have compared Cognos Workspace Advanced to Query Studio and Analysis Studio. We have also looked at how to use the tool both from a basic and advanced perspective. With Cognos Workspace Advanced, you now have a one-stop shop for reporting and analysis for business users.

In the next chapter, we will look at the interfaces for developers and administrators within Cognos BI. We will begin by exploring Cognos Report Studio and discovering the most advanced report development tool for IBM Cognos BI.

8
IBM Cognos Report Studio

If Cognos Query Studio, Cognos Analysis Studio, and Cognos Workspace Advanced are the corner bakery, the meat store, and the cheese shop of business intelligence, then Cognos Report Studio is the super store (fill in the blank with your favorite). While Cognos Query Studio, Cognos Analysis Studio, and Cognos Workspace Advanced all have the necessary tools to accomplish the goals of the specific processes, they don't have a complete, pixel-perfect reporting capability. Cognos Report Studio has it all; advanced query writing, the ability to create pixel-perfect reports, complete customization, and so much more. In this chapter we will look at:

- Who should use Cognos Report Studio
- Accessing Cognos Report Studio
- Cognos Report Studio report types
- The drag-and-drop interface and the right-click menu
- The properties pane
- Building Active Reports
- The business case for Cognos Report Studio

Who should use Cognos Report Studio

Cognos Report Studio is designed for professional report developers. These are the people that make reports that can be published in quarterly reports, sent to stock holders, or used for published reports. The product can accommodate the creation of simpler, non-professional report development as well. Professional report development is both a highly technical and a highly business-minded activity. The ideal candidate for performing this type of task will be able to quickly grasp new technology as well as understand business needs.

Despite the need for a strong business understanding, developers will often sit in an IT group. Many organizations have entire **Business Intelligence** (**BI**) teams that roll up under IT, and it is these groups that perform the report development task.

In addition to a core BI team, many larger organizations also have a **Business Intelligence Competency Center** (**BICC**) or **Business Intelligence Center of Excellence** (**BICOE**) groups. These groups are made up of all stakeholders, which will typically include a BI team as well as power users within the business departments. In these situations, you will usually have one or more Cognos Report Studio users within the specific business units.

Accessing Cognos Report Studio

You can access Cognos Report Studio in the same ways that we have accessed the other studios; from the **Welcome** page or from the **Launch** menu.

To access it from the **Welcome** page, we can choose the option **Author advanced reports**:

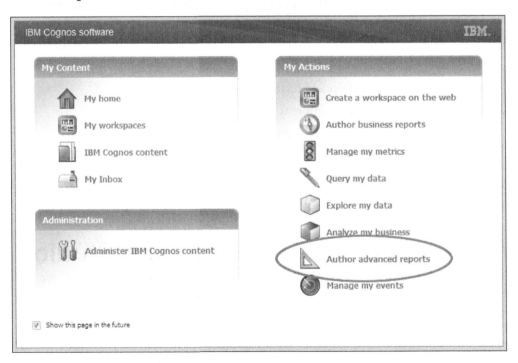

The other way to access Cognos Report Studio is through **Launch | Report Studio**:

You will then be prompted to choose a package from which you will develop your advanced report. For the sake of an example, we will select the same Cognos sample package **Go Sales and Retailers**, that we used for Analysis Studio. This is built from the Cognos Great Outdoors PowerCube.

When the tool is first launched, you will be greeted with a splash screen that has two buttons: **Create new** and **Open existing**. You can choose either of these buttons accordingly to start working with your reports.

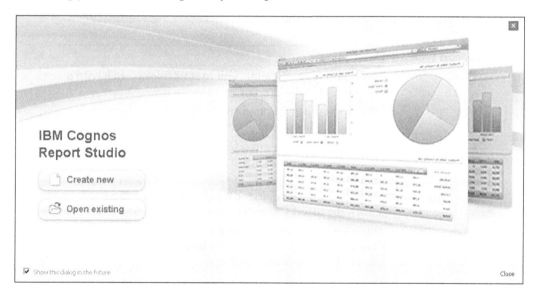

We will create a new report, which will bring us to a list of the standard report types.

Cognos Report Studio report types

When you first start a new report, you will be presented with a list of report types. The reports types available are:

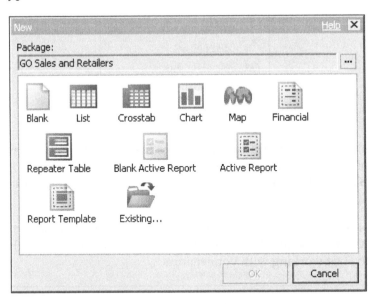

Report type	Description
Blank	This report type will allow you to start from scratch with a completely blank slate.
List	This report type will provide a header and footer section plus a single **List** object in your body.
Crosstab	This report type will provide a header and footer section plus a single **Crosstab** object in your body.
Chart	This report type will provide a header and footer section plus a single **Chart** object in your body. This will also launch the **Insert Chart** dialogue.
Map	This report type will provide a header and footer section plus a single **Map** object in your body. This will also launch the **Choose Map** dialogue.
Financial	This report type will provide a header and footer section plus a single **Financial Crosstab** object in your body. This allows you to build financial style reports with default standard formatting.

Report type	Description
Statistical (not shown)	This report type will provide a header and footer section plus a single **Statistical** object in your body. This will also launch the **Statistical Chart Creation** dialog.
Repeater Table	This report type will provide a header and footer section plus a **Repeater Table** object in your body. A repeater table allows you to repeat the table for each row of data from one of your query items. This works great for things where you want to repeat what you are showing on each page of a report (for instance, showing a full page of information for each month in your data).
Blank Active Report	This report type will provide a header and footer section with a blank area for creating Active Report. Choosing this option opens up additional insertable objects that are specific to Active Reports.
Active Report	This report type will provide a header and footer section with a template for creating an Active Report. Choosing this option opens up additional insertable objects that are specific to Active Reports.
Report Template	This report type will provide a header and footer section plus a single **List** object in your body. It will also add a filter icon to the report at the top. This tool is used for creating query studio templates.
Existing	This option will allow you to open an existing report.

For the sake of example, we will select **Blank** and begin building our report from scratch.

The drag-and-drop interface and the right-click menu

Cognos Report Studio has the most advanced drag-and-drop interface and right-click menu of all of the studios. As a result, it is also the most powerful studio.

Understanding the different areas in Cognos Report Studio

Cognos Report Studio is broken up into different sections for different tasks. In the following screenshot we can see those at a high level:

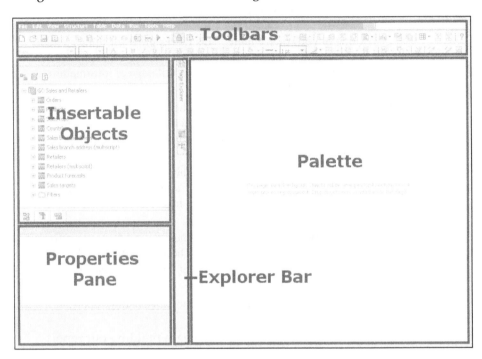

The top-most section is the toolbars section. This is where many of your insert and edit tasks are. It is also where you can go to open or save a report, lock certain report objects, change views, and carry out a number of other actions on your report.

The left-most section at the top is the **Insertable Objects** pane. This is where you can drag items from your package into the report for the first time, drag existing items from queries into your report, or drag in other page objects that make up the different parts of your report.

Below the **Insertable Objects** pane is your **Properties** pane. The **Properties** pane is one of the major differentiators between Cognos Report Studio and the other Studios. This section allows you to make changes to how objects look and behave on the page down to the pixel level.

The large, lower-right section is the palette. Think of this as your canvas, where you will construct your report from blank slate to masterpiece.

The area between the left-hand panes and the palette is your explorer bar. Within this bar are the **Page Explorer**, **Query Explorer**, and **Condition Explorer** panes.

The **Page Explorer** pane allows you to move between report and prompt pages:

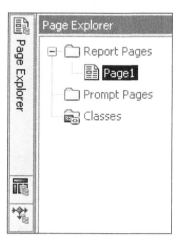

The **Query Explorer** pane allows you to move directly to the underlying **Queries** section and edit them. This is also where you can go to add queries with custom SQL or MDX:

The **Condition Explorer** pane allows you to create report variables that will change the behavior of the report based on variable conditions:

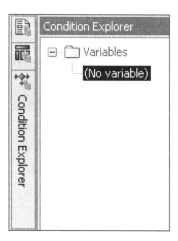

We will explore each of these sections in more detail later in the chapter.

Adding objects to your report

With Cognos Report Studio, we have a section known as the **Insertable Objects** pane. The **Insertable Objects** pane contains objects that can be dragged to your palette. These objects include objects from your package, objects from an existing query, and objects from the toolbox. It is a good idea to create the outline of your report by dragging objects to the palette from the toolbox. There are many objects available within the toolbox, and they are as follows:

- **Text item**: This object allows you to add static or dynamic text to a page. **Static text** would be anything that the developer writes. **Dynamic text** would be based on the data or a selected variable from within the report.

- **Block**: This object allows you to create sections or groups within your report. Because blocks can be formatted or set to conditionally change, this is a very useful object for organizing the layout of your page.

- **Table**: This object allows you to add a table to your page. Tables are most often used for organizing your page. Tables can contain any other type of object within them.

- **Field set**: This object is very similar to a block object, but it also allows you to add text at the top of the object that shows on the report. These can also be very useful in organizing your page.

- **Query calculation**: This object is used to add a new item to your query that is based on a calculation. A new data item will be created automatically in the query.

- **Layout calculation**: This object allows you to add a calculated item based on report functions. Report functions will allow you to create a calculation based on when the report is run. Page number or run time are examples of report functions. You may use this object to create a calculation to show yesterday's date by choosing the report expression **Today()** and subtracting 1.

- **Intersection (tuple)**: This object allows you to display the point at which multiple dimensions and measures meet. This intersection of data is also called a tuple.

- **Image**: This object allows you to insert an image. The image must be accessible from the web at the time the report is run or must be installed within the designated image folder of your IBM Cognos BI v10 installation (typically `<install location>/IBM/webcontent/samples/images/`).

- **Crosstab space**: This object allows you to add a spacer into a crosstab.

- **Crosstab space (with fact cells)**: This object allows you to add a spacer with text or data information into a crosstab.

- **List**: This object allows you to add a list to your report. A list is simply a list of information from your data in a table format.

- **Crosstab**: This object allows you to add a crosstab to your report. A crosstab is an object that shows data points for multiple dimensions at once (typically two).

- **Chart**: This object allows you to add a chart to your report. There are many chart options that will be displayed when this object is dragged to the palette.

- **Map**: This object allows you to add a map to your report. There are many maps available natively in IBM Cognos BI v10. In addition, you can purchase additional maps from the supplier of the mapping capabilities (MapInfo). IBM Cognos BI v10 also ships with a tool for creating your own maps called Map Manager.

- **Repeater table**: This object allows you to repeat items on a page in a table structure using the information from your data. This is typically used for mailing labels or anything that you would want to repeat.

- **Repeater**: This object allows you to repeat items on a page, without a particular structure, using the information from your data. This is typically used for mailing labels or anything that you would want to repeat.

- **Singleton**: This object allows you to add a single piece of information to a report from your data. It will run a query to pull back the first row of information when a query is executed. You typically see this used in conjunction with filters to bring back relevant information for a report. A good example would be if you wanted to show a transaction date at the top of an invoice report, you could bring in a singleton using that data item.

- **Conditional blocks**: This object allows you to create different report objects based on a variable condition. First, a variable is set on your conditional blocks. Then, you can choose what to show within the block when each option from that variable is true.

- **HTML item**: This object allows you to insert HTML into your report that is executed when the report is run in HTML or MHT format. HTML items can include JavaScript for determining how a report runs or just basic HTML for adding additional formatting to a report. This is a very powerful object that allows you to truly customize the report interaction experience.

- **Rich text item**: This object allows you to display some HTML in a report. The power of this item is that it works with HTML, MHT, and PDF. The text can be dynamic or static.

- **Hyperlink**: This object allows you to display a link within your report.

- **Hyperlink button**: This object allows you to display a link within your report that is accessed by clicking on a button object.

- **Date**: This object allows you to insert the runtime date into the report.

- **Time**: This object allows you to insert the runtime into the report.

- **As of time expression**: This object allows you to create a new expression for what the date and time objects will display. For instance, if you change this expression to `_add_Days(ReportDate(), -1)`, you will display the runtime date as one day prior to the actual date the report was run on. This can be useful in scheduled reporting that has to wait for data to load.

- **Page number**: This object allows you to add a page number to any or all pages in a report.

- **Row number**: This object allows you to add row numbers to the list or crosstab objects.

- **Layout component reference**: This object allows you to add an object or group of objects that have been created in the same report or another report by using the name given to those objects within the **Properties** pane.

- **Metric studio diagram**: This object allows you to add a metric studio diagram to your report as an image. You can set this to be static, based on the point it was created, or dynamic and update it with each run. These are often used to link Metric Studio KPIs back to a report.

The following items are available only in Active Reports:

- **Variable text item**: This object allows you to display the value of an Active Report variable on a report.
- **Deck**: This object allows you to create a custom set of cards that will be displayed based on a changing variable. The variable labels are defined by the developer.
- **Data deck**: This object allows you to create a custom set of cards that will be displayed based on a changing variable. The variable labels are defined by the data.
- **Tab control**: This object allows the end user to tab through different sets of information on tabs that are defined by the developer. Tab control also includes an area where objects are inserted.
- **Data tab control**: This object allows the end user to tab through different sets of information on tabs that are defined by the data. Tab control also includes an area where objects are inserted.
- **Button bar**: This object allows the end user to click between different sets of information on buttons that are defined by the developer. A button does not include an area where objects are inserted.
- **Data button bar**: This object allows the end user to click between different sets of information on buttons that are defined by the data. A button does not include an area where objects are inserted.
- **Toggle button bar**: This object allows the end user to click between different sets of information on buttons that are defined by the developer. A button does not include an area where objects are inserted. A toggle button bar item differs from a button bar item in that it allows the selection of multiple buttons at once.
- **Data toggle button bar**: This object allows the end user to click between different sets of information on buttons that are defined by the data. A button does not include an area where objects are inserted. A data toggle button bar item differs from a button bar item in that it allows the selection of multiple buttons at once.

- **Radio button group**: This object allows the use of radio button selection within Active Report. The radio button selection can then be used to filter your report. The options are defined by the developer.

- **Data radio button group**: This object allows the use of a radio button selection within Active Report. The radio button selection can then be used to filter your report. The options are defined by the data.

- **Check box group**: This object allows the use of a checkbox option for selecting multiple items at once. The options in the checkbox are defined by the developer.

- **Data check box group**: This object allows the use of a checkbox option for selecting multiple items at once. The options in the checkbox are defined by the data.

- **Drop-down list**: This object allows the use of a drop-down list option for selecting an option from a drop-down menu. The options in the drop-down menu are defined by the developer.

- **Data drop-down list**: This object allows the use of a drop-down list option for selecting an option from a drop-down menu. The options in the drop-down menu are defined by the data.

- **List box**: This object allows the use of a list box for selecting multiple items to filter on. The options in the list box are defined by the developer.

- **Data list box**: This object allows the use of a list box for selecting multiple items to filter on. The options in the list box are defined by the data.

- **Button**: This option allows you to add a button to your page. The button can then interact with various variables in Active Report.

When adding objects to your palette, it is important to consider the layout first. We can do this by asking ourselves, "What needs to be included in this report and how can I best represent it?". Best practice should be to then add a series of tables and/or blocks to break up your page into the different sections that you would like to have depicted on the report.

For the sake of an example, we will create a report for a U.S. sales manager. This manager wants to see how his sales are compared to other countries' sales . He would also like to see the details of how he is doing in each state. To accomplish this, we will develop a report that has four separate report objects. We will include a list object, a combination chart, a map, and a drill-based list report that is fed from the map. Our first step with this example will be to break up our palette into four equal parts by dragging in a two-by-two table:

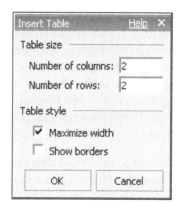

We can now populate each section with the objects that we intend to use in the report. We will drag a list object to the upper-left quadrant, a column chart to the upper-right quadrant, a map object to the lower-left quadrant (when we are prompted, we can choose a map of the Continental U.S.), and an additional list object to the lower-right quadrant.

We now have the basic outline of what will become of our report:

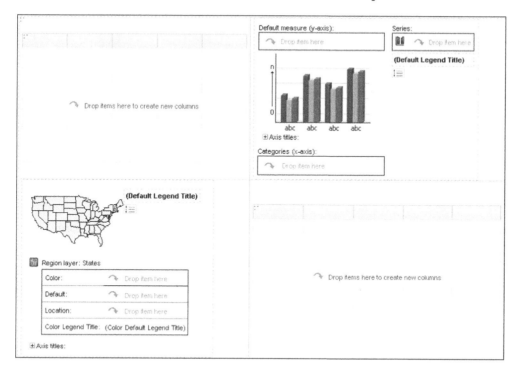

Before we move to adding data into our report, it is important to always name all of our objects in Cognos Report Studio. As we begin working with Active Reports later in this chapter, or as end users begin interacting with our reports in other tools such as Cognos Office or Business Insight, the names of these objects are used to determine what objects should be utilized in those tools. Therefore, we need to name our objects and queries. To do this, highlight an entire object by selecting the three grey dots in the upper-left corner. Then, in the **Properties** pane, scroll to the bottom where you see the property **Name**. Here you can set the name to anything that you like.

For the sake of future users, it is best to provide a descriptive name for your objects. We will select our first list and rename it from **List1** to **Country Sales Information List**:

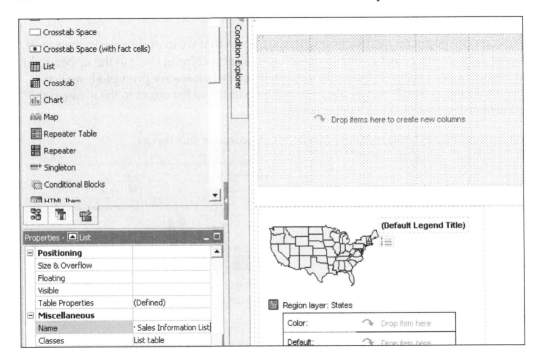

This is also a good opportunity to call out the importance of planning before developing. If you know what you will be designing and putting into your report prior to building it, you will have an easier time naming your objects and queries.

Our next step will be to go to the corresponding query for the list that we have renamed. Hover over the **Query Explorer** pane and choose **Query1**:

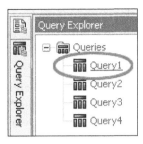

Again, we will scroll to the bottom of the **Properties** pane to find the **Name** property and we will change it from **Query1** to **CountrySalesQuery**:

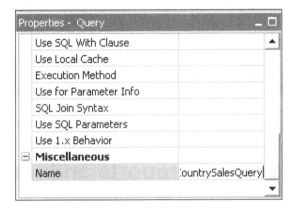

Note that we are using a different naming convention here by leaving out spaces. It is best to adopt a naming convention that will make it easier for you to understand what each object does during your development process. I have always used spaces for page objects and removed spaces on queries. You may choose to adopt this naming convention or use a different one that will be easier for you to adopt.

Next, we will repoint the chart in the upper-right corner to the **Query** table that we have just renamed. We can do this by selecting the chart in the upper-right hand corner and then changing the drop-down menu to repoint from **Query2** to **CountrySalesQuery**:

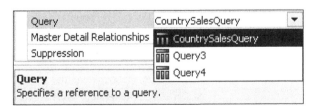

We will now proceed to change the names of each of our additional objects and corresponding queries. In doing so, we will use the naming conventions as shown in the following table:

Object	Original name	New name	Original query	New query
Upper-left list	**List1**	**Country Sales Information List**	**Query1**	**CountrySalesQuery**
Upper-right chart	**Chart1**	**Country Sales Information Chart**	**Query2**	**Re-point the chart to CountrySalesQuery**
Lower-left map	**Map1**	**US Sales Map**	**Query3**	**USSalesMapQuery**
Lower-left list	**List2**	**State Sales List**	**Query4**	**StateSalesQuery**

In the next section we will add data to our report within each report object.

Adding data to your reports and formatting

The next step is to add data to each of our report objects. We will start with the list in the upper-left hand corner. Drag in the following items:

- **Countries | Country**
- **Orders | Revenue**
- **Orders | Planned revenue**
- **Orders | Quantity**

Next, select **Revenue** and **Planned revenue** and right-click on it. Now, go to **Calculate | % Difference (Revenue, Planned revenue)**:

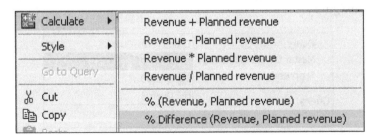

We will now go to the **Name** property in the **Properties** pane, and change the **Name** field to **Revenue Variance**.

When this has been done, our list will look like this:

Country	Revenue	Planned revenue	Revenue Variance	Quantity
<Country>	<Revenue>	<Planned revenue>	<Revenue Variance>	<Quantity>
<Country>	<Revenue>	<Planned revenue>	<Revenue Variance>	<Quantity>
<Country>	<Revenue>	<Planned revenue>	<Revenue Variance>	<Quantity>

When we run the report, we see that Revenue and Planned Revenue are both formatted as currency with two decimal places. Select Revenue and Planned Revenue. We can change the formatting by pressing *Ctrl* and clicking on the **List Column Body** section below each of those items. We can then update formatting by either going to the **Properties** pane and selecting **Data Format** or by clicking on the **Data Format** icon in the toolbar area:

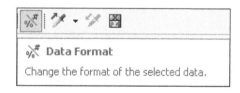

Once the **Data Format** dialog comes up, we will choose **Currency** for our **Format type** field and **0** for our **No. of Decimal Places** field:

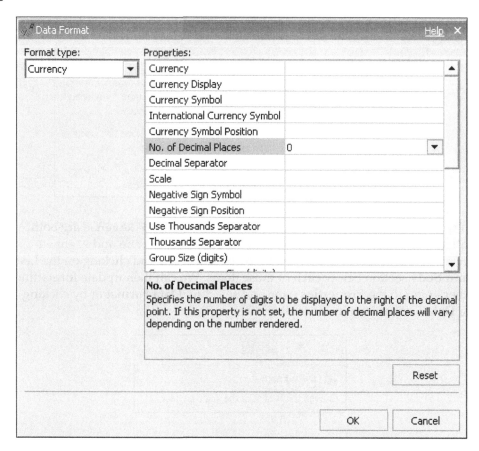

In order to limit the amount of data that is pulled back, let's add a rank and a filter to our query. Right-click on the list and choose **Go to Query**. Select **Revenue**, and in the **Properties** area, change the **Pre-Sort** property to **Sort descending**.

Drag a filter in and type `Rank([Revenue]) <= 5`. With the filter still selected, change the **Application** property to **After Auto Aggregation**:

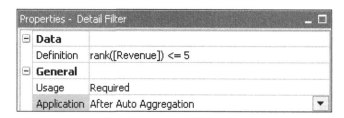

This will limit our report to only return the top five companies by revenue.

We will now set up the chart in the upper-right corner to reflect the same information. Since we have already changed **Query1** to **CountrySalesQuery**, we can pull from that query and add it to the chart object. We will drag **Country** to **Categories** (on the x axis), **Revenue** to **Series**, and **Quantity** to **Series** (below **Revenue**). We will then select **Quantity** from the chart. In the **Properties** area, set the **Axis Assignment** field to **Y2 Axis** and the **Chart Type** field to **Line**:

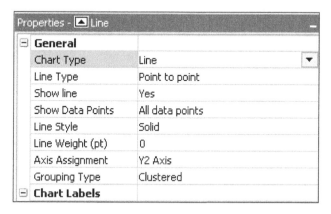

This will create a separate axis for our two different measures. We will now select the legend image within our chart and set our **Position** field to **Bottom**:

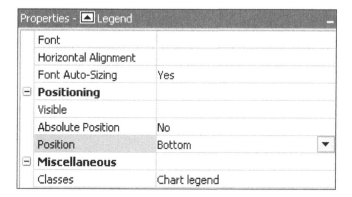

Now that we have set up our report to include worldwide information, we can focus the lower two sections just on the U.S.. For the map, we will drag **Orders | Quantity** to our **Color** field and **Retailers | Region** to our **Location** field:

Select the entire chart, and in the **Properties** area, set the **Ignore Data with No Features** property to **Yes**. This will hide information from our data that cannot be added to the chart.

If we run our report, we will see that we have our top-five countries at the top and that we have our map in the lower-left corner. Unfortunately, the palette is off, so our map looks almost entirely red:

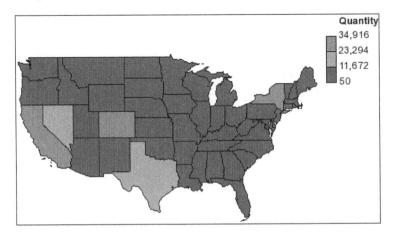

Back in Cognos Report Studio, select the area that says **Region layer: States** by clicking on it. In the **Properties** area, there is a blank area to the right of the **Palette** field. Click on the white space to the right of that and then click on the ellipsis that appears:

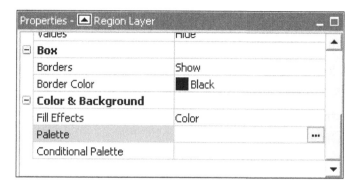

In the **Palette** dialogue, leave **Discrete Colors** selected, uncheck **Percentage**, change **66.66**% to **10000**, and change **33.33**% to **1000**:

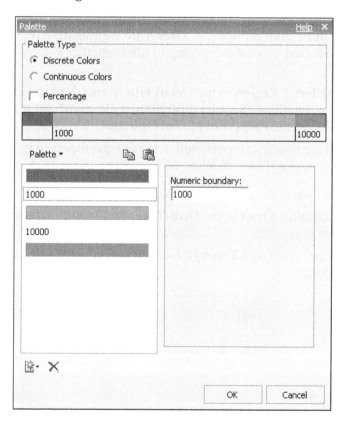

Our map report will now look more balanced.

Finally, let's focus on the list in the lower-right corner. In this list, we want to focus on our top ranked cities in the U.S.. We also want to link back to the map so that we can filter to a state that is clicked on.

To do so, perform the following steps:

1. To start, let's drag in the following:
    ◦ **Retailers | City**
    ◦ **Orders | Revenue**
    ◦ **Orders | Planned revenue**
    ◦ **Orders | Quantity**

2. Right-click on the list and choose **Go to Query**. Choose **Revenue** and set **Pre-Sort** to **Sort descending**.

3. Drag in a new filter and add **gosales_goretailers].[Countries].[Country] = 'United States'**. Also, drag in a new filter and add **Rank([Revenue]) <= 5**.

4. Set the **Application** property to **After Auto Aggregation** on your new filter. Finally, we need to set the query up to filter whether a state is selected in the map.

5. Drag **Retailers | Region** to the **Detail Filters** area. Edit the filter to say **[gosales_goretailers].[Retailers].[Region] = ?Region?**. Set the **Usage** field on this filter in the **Properties** area to **Optional**.

    Now that we have our report built, let's save the report to My Folders as Example Report. This will allow us to perform our next step.

6. Select the map in the lower-left corner and set up a drill-through.

7. Choose the ellipsis next to the **Drill-Through Definitions** property in the **Properties** pane.

8. Click on the **New Drill-Through Definition** button to add a drill-through to the report:

9. Choose the report that we just saved as our drill-through report. Then, click on the **Edit** option under **Parameters**.

10. In the **Parameters** dialogue we can choose a **Method** item of **Pass data item value** and a **Value** item of **Region**. Click on **OK** twice and save your report. If you want to run the report now and click on a few states, you can see how the report is updated with the cities for the states that you click on.

Exploring your queries with Query Explorer

We can now explore our underlying queries by selecting **Query Explorer** in the explorer pane and then selecting **Queries**:

Our **Insertable Objects** options in our **Query Explorer** pane are:

- **Query**: This will create a new query for us
- **Join**: This will create a join between two different queries
- **Union**: This will bring two queries together that have commonly named data items
- **Intersect**: This option will show the common rows of data between two queries
- **Except**: This option will allow us to either remove or identify duplicates between two queries
- **SQL**: This option will allow us to create a new query from custom-written SQL
- **MDX**: This option will allow us to create a new query from custom-written MDX

Setting up conditions

We can set up variables by selecting **Condition Explorer** | **Variables**:

We will see three types of variables available:

- **Report language variable**: This variable will allow you to set up a variable that contains different languages. It will prompt you to choose which languages to include in the variable.

- **String variable**: This variable will allow you to write an expression and manually define the possible values for that expression.

- **Boolean variable**: This variable will allow you to write an expression whose values can only be Yes or No.

For our purposes, we can drag in a new Boolean variable and type in `ParamCount('Region')>0` to create a Yes or No variable that tells us whether a state has been clicked on. Just to keep up with the practice of naming our objects, we will change our **Name** property to **StateSelected?** from **Boolean1**.

We now go back to our page, select our entire list in the lower-right corner, and click on the ellipsis next to the **Render Variable** property. We will then choose **StateSelected?** from the drop-down menu. We need to make sure that **Yes** is selected and then click on **OK**.

Now, if we save and re-run, you will see that the list does not show up until a state is selected. This is a very common way of using conditional variables.

Adding a prompt to filter results

Prompts are very useful tools that allow us to filter our data based on a user-selected parameter. For our report, we are going to add a prompt that will filter our results based on which sales reps are associated with our sales numbers. The easiest way to do this is by selecting what we would like to add the parameter to and then clicking on the filter icon at the top. We can select our map and then click on the drop-down arrow on the filter icon. We will then choose **Edit Filters...**:

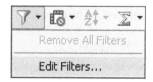

Within the filter editor, click on the icon in the lower left-hand corner to add a filter, and then select **Advanced** and click on **OK**:

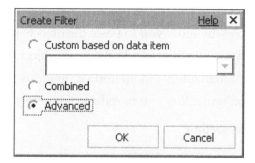

Next, drag in **Sales reps | Staff name** and then type in ?Staff?. Your total filter should read as [gosales_goretailers].[Sales reps].[Staff name] in ?Staff?. By putting Staff within question marks, you are creating a parameter named Staff. By using the operator in, you are saying that this is a multi-select parameter. Now, if we run the report, IBM Cognos BI will automatically generate a prompt that allows us to select multiple members of the sales staff. It will then filter our query behind the map to only include data for those members of the sales staff.

Understanding the other buttons

Now that we understand how to create a basic report with drill-through, let's look at our other buttons. We will look at them in groups.

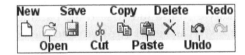

In our first section we have the following buttons:

- **New**: This will create a new report
- **Open**: This option will open an existing report
- **Save**: This option will allow you to save your report
- **Cut**: This option will allow you to cut an object or series of objects
- **Copy**: This option will allow you to create a copy of an object or a series of objects
- **Paste**: This option will allow you to paste the objects that are cut or copied
- **Delete**: This option will allow you to delete an object or series of objects
- **Undo**: This option will allow you to undo a previous action
- **Redo**: This option will allow you to redo a previously undone action

Here is a view of the next section:

In this section we have the following buttons:

- **Validate**: This button will validate the report specifications for your report
- **XML**: This report will show the XML specifications for your report
- **Play**: This option will run your report
- **Lock**: This option will lock or unlock your report objects so that you can edit within report objects
- **Visual Aids**: This option will allow you to see or hide visual aids on your report that help you design your report

- **Back**: This option takes you to the previous area of Cognos Report Studio that was open
- **Forward**: This option takes you forward after using the back button
- **Up**: This option takes you up a level from the area of Cognos Report Studio you are in
- **Filter**: This option allows you to add a filter to a report
- **Suppress**: This option allows you to suppress zeros on columns or rows
- **Sort**: This option allows you to sort a column either in ascending or descending order
- **Summary**: This option allows you to create a summary row within a list or crosstab
- **Calculate**: This option allows you to create a new calculation on multiple list or crosstab options

Here is a view of the next section:

In this section we have the following buttons:

- **Group**: This option will allow you to group data by column
- **Pivot**: This option will allow you to pivot from a list to a crosstab moving the items selected to the top of the crosstab
- **Section**: This option will create sections based on the data item selected
- **Swap**: This option will switch columns and rows out with each other in a crosstab
- **Headers/Footers**: This option will allow you to create headers and footers on the report or in a list
- **Chart**: This option will allow you to add a chart to the report
- **Prompt**: This option will allow you to create a prompt page automatically based on filter parameters
- **Drill**: This option will allow you to create a drill-through to another report
- **Table**: This option will allow you to add a table to a report

- **Merge**: This option will allow you to merge two or more cells into one
- **Split**: This option will allow you to split merged cells back into multiple cells
- **Help**: This option will launch the Cognos Report Studio User Guide

Building Active Reports

An Active Report is a report that can be consumed offline. We looked at how end users can interact with Active Reports in *Chapter 3, IBM Cognos Active Reports*. Here, we will look at how these reports are created using Cognos Report Studio.

Designing your Active Report

The first step to a successful Active Report is determining what information you want to display and how you will display it. The design phase of Active Report development is the most important as it will create our roadmap for when we get to the technical aspects of development.

A few questions that you may want to ask are as follows:

- What information will my end users want to see offline?
- How can I best display that information?
- Are there logical ways to break up this information?
- If my information is hierarchical, what is a typical drillpath?
- Who will be using this information?
- How often will it need to be refreshed?

These questions can go on and on. The important thing is to fully understand your end goal before you get started.

What I recommend doing as an exercise, is drawing out on a piece of paper or in a designing tool, such as Visio, exactly how you want your report to look and what interactivity you would like to add. You can then work with your end users to determine whether the information that you are planning to make available is relevant to their needs and whether it would be valuable to have the information available to them while disconnected. Remember that too much information can be a bad thing with Active Reports. The more information that you store in the report, the larger the file becomes, and the more difficult it becomes to distribute.

As an example, let us assume that our end users have asked for a report that shows the percentage returns by state. We will later learn that they would also like to be able to drill into a state to see the percentage of returns per store.

If we were to begin drawing out how this would look, we would want to start with an easy to follow way of displaying return percentage by state. We could argue that a map object would be the best option here.

We would then begin considering how to graphically display return percentages. It is best to work with your end users at this phase to determine what the typical return percentages are, what their targets are, and what return percentages are considered too high. We will use these thresholds as our color indicators. For the sake of our example, let's assume that 1 percent or less is our goal return percentage and less than 5 percent is acceptable.

Choosing the Active Report component to use

After deciding how to display our information, we should decide which components to use on the report. All Active Report components are used to make a report interactive during offline use. We can start by dragging in a **Map** object to the report. Select the **Continental 48 US map** option. Since we will be passing information from the map to a **List** object, we need to set up an Active Report component to hold our **List** object. Below our **Map** object, drag in a **Data Deck** item from the **Insertable Objects** area:

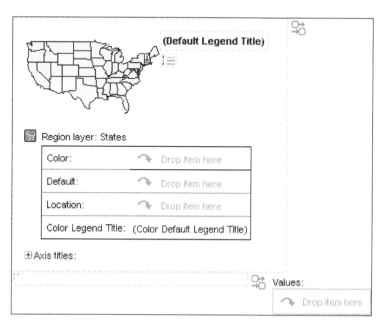

Finally, drag a **List** object into the **Data Deck** item to complete the layout of our new Active Report, as shown in the following screenshot, and perform the following steps:

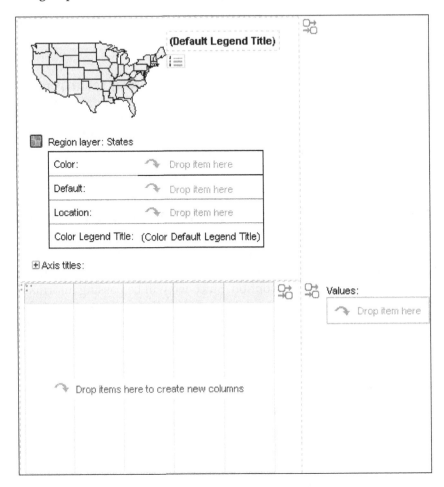

1. We can populate our **Map** object by dragging in **Retailers | Region** as our **Location** field.

2. We will then drag in a new **Query Calculation** item from **Insertable Objects** and give it the name e `Return Percent`.

3. We will use the expression [gosales_goretailers].[Orders].[Return quantity]/[gosales_goretailers].[Orders].[Quantity]. We will then change the **Aggregate Function** and **Rollup Aggregate Function** fields to **Calculated**.

4. We then need to update our palette. To do this, we will select the area of the **Map** object that says **Region layer: States**.

5. Next, choose the ellipsis next to the **Palette** property. Then, choose the **Three Color Reversed** palette from the **Palette** drop-down menu:

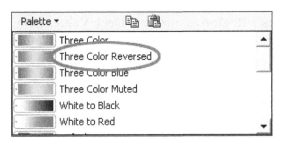

6. We will then change **Palette Type** to **Discrete Colors** and uncheck **Percentage**. We will then change our numeric boundary for the first threshold to 0.01 and the second threshold to 0.05:

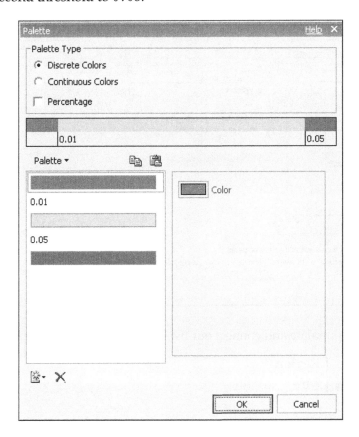

7. Back on our main page, we need to do a bit of cleaning up and renaming. We will rename our **Map** object to **ReturnPercentMap**. We will also set **Ignore Data with No Features** to **Yes**.

Let's focus next on our Data Deck item and perform the following steps:

1. Drag **Retailers | Region** as our **Data Deck Values** item. Select the entire **Data Deck** item by choosing the dots in the upper-left corner.

2. Set the **Name** property to **RegionDetails_DataDeck**.

3. Now, click on **Interactive Behavior** to bring up a dialog for creating our connection from our map to our data deck.

4. In the dialog, select **Create a New Connection...** to build a connection between our two objects.

5. Build the connection from **ReturnPercentMap** to **RegionDetails_DataDeck** with **Region** for the **Data Item** field on both objects. Also, name the new variable that we are creating **RegionVariable**:

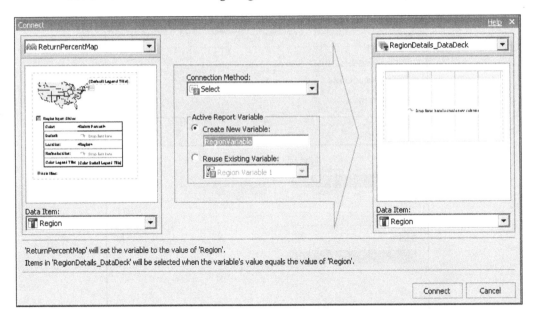

Finally, we will populate and connect our list to the map. Populate the **List** object with:

- **Retailers | Region**
- **Retailers | City**

- For **Query Calculation** enter the following data in the corresponding fields:

    ○ **Name**: Return Percent

    ○ **Expression Definition**: [gosales_goretailers].[Orders].[Return quantity]/[gosales_goretailers].[Orders].[Quantity]

    ○ **Aggregate Function**: Calculated

    ○ **Rollup Aggregate Function**: Calculated

Next, we will format **Return Percent** in both the **Map** and **List** objects to **Percent**:

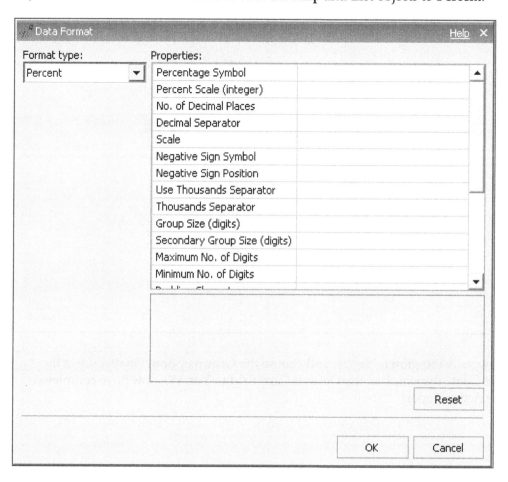

Select the entire list and choose the ellipsis to the right-hand side of the **Master Detail Relationships** property. Create a new link between **Region** and **Region**:

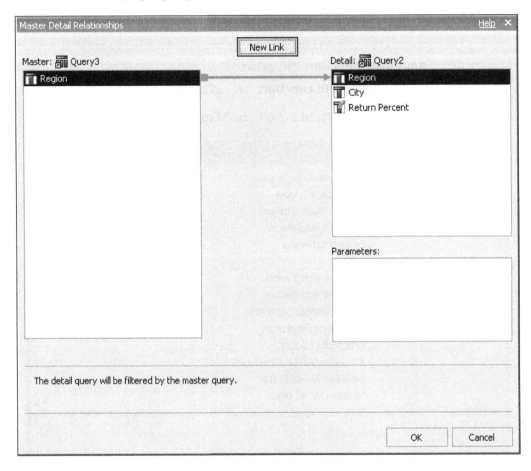

Now, select **Region** in the list and choose the **Group** option. Finally, select the entire data deck and set the **Default Card** field to **Yes**. We now have completed our Active Report:

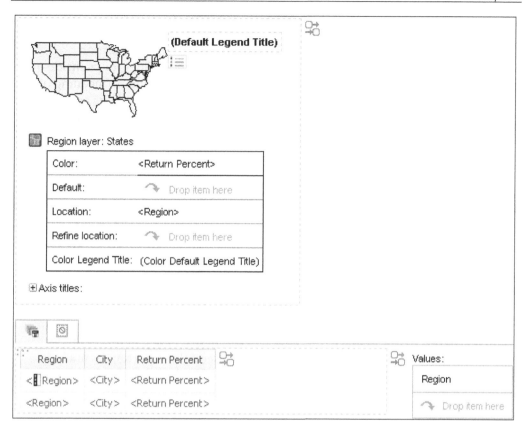

When we run the report, we will see that our map has a nice variety of colors, and if we click on a state, we can see the return percent for each city.

The business case for Cognos Report Studio

Cognos Report Studio is a tool that is designed for building advanced, complicated, and production-worthy reports. Any business that has a need for this type of report will need access to Cognos Report Studio. You can often think of these as reports that are going to be shared outside of your organization or that have been developed for internal end users. Cognos Report Studio is also used many times for developing advanced reports that are used within an organization. In the following sections we will discuss how each of these two areas might use Cognos Report Studio.

Reporting inside of the organization

We often see Cognos Report Studio used to report inside the organization. Unfortunately, this audience is often overlooked. Most reporting groups inside of an organization have their primary customers as internal customers (meaning other employees within different groups of their organization). In order to be an effective report developer, it is important to understand who your customers are and what information would be most important to them.

Cognos Report Studio is an advanced reporting tool. Therefore, it is not something that you typically see in the hands of business users. The Cognos Report Studio developer's role is to bridge the gap between the business user, who understands the business and the information that is relevant to them, and the technology that has been designed to present this information in a meaningful way. In order to be effective at that, you need to understand what types of reports present certain data well.

By working with Cognos Report Studio often, you begin to realize what types of information will be better presented in one form or another. For instance, if I want to show sales growth or loss by region year-over-year, I know that a line chart or a column chart would be effective, because of their ability to depict time visually. Your internal clients will look up to you to understand the reporting technology. You will need to utilize their expertise to understand their data and what they want to see from it.

Reporting outside of the organization

We often see Cognos Report Studio used to develop reports that are going outside of an organization as well. With Cognos being a web-based application, it makes perfect sense to be able to place reports on a web server outside of a company firewall and provide reports to external clients or stakeholders. I personally have seen this type of reporting provided in the following ways. This list is by no means all-inclusive:

- Insurance companies providing reports to individuals on their insurance usage as well as to companies on their group activity
- Banks providing reports on account activity through their online banking system
- Publicly-traded companies using Cognos Report Studio to design their monthly, quarterly, and annual reports
- Electric companies using Cognos Report Studio to design distributed reports that show electricity usage

- Direct sales companies using Cognos Report Studio to design invoices
- Healthcare companies using Cognos Report Studio to send out regulatory reports

In addition to these ways, there are hundreds of other uses for Cognos Report Studio that we could not possibly touch on in one chapter. The more you use it, the more you will begin to see your own use cases.

Summary

In this chapter we have looked at Cognos Report Studio and how to create reports within it. We explored which users are best suited for Cognos Report Studio and how to access it. We looked at the different types of reports that can be created and how to create them. We explored the power of the **Properties** pane and even built an Active Report. We wrapped up the chapter by looking at the business case for Cognos Report Studio.

In the next chapter we will look at building models in Framework Manager. We will explore Metadata Wizard and look at best practices for creating and maintaining metadata.

9
IBM Cognos Framework Manager

This chapter will take a deeper dive into the concept of metadata. In it, we will look at the best practices of designs for Cognos Framework Manager models and what type of user would be best suited for model design:

- Introduction to metadata
- Managing the model design project
- 3-tier approach to model design
- Designing a database view of data
- Designing a business view of data
- Designing an end user view of data
- The business case for Cognos Framework Manager

Introduction to metadata

We looked at metadata from an end user perspective when we were first introduced to our studios. In this chapter, we will look at it from the design side.

To recap, metadata is the data that tells you about your other data. Metadata can include descriptions of your data, information on how to transform your data, or formatting information for your data. There are three basic types of metadata, namely, technical, business, and process.

- **Technical metadata**: Metadata of this type is used to describe the technical aspects of the data or data containers. Examples of this type of metadata would include things such as the original data formatting, database expression, or data type.

- **Business metadata**: Metadata of this type is used to describe the business aspects of the data or data containers. Examples of this type of metadata would include things such as the logical name of a data item, a description of the data item, or a screen tip that could be displayed while interacting with a data item.

- **Process metadata**: Metadata of this type is used to describe the processing aspects of the data or data containers. Examples of this type of metadata would include things such as calculations that are performed on the data before displaying it, reformatting of data that takes place, and relationships that tie multiple tables of data together.

With Cognos Framework Manager, you create and manage each of these types of metadata. Each type serves a different purpose; however, each type is very important to the overall functionality of your final Cognos package.

A package is the end result of designing a Cognos Framework Manager model. Once all of the metadata is defined, a package is published to Cognos Connection, and that package contains all of the metadata within it. Then, when a developer or an end user interacts with that package, the metadata tells Cognos how to display the data, where to pull it from, and how to transform it.

Managing the model design project

In order to design an effective model, you need to first understand the business case for the model. Once you understand the business case, you should be able to determine where the necessary data is coming from and successfully complete your project if you follow a few basic rules.

Rule 1 – gather information

We should know where to gather business information and where to gather technical information.

During the information-gathering phase of a new project, it can be very easy to choose one person or group of people within the business community or technical community and only focus on them. In reality, every project will have different stakeholders and each stakeholder will be able to provide a different type of information. If you work with multiple areas of the business to gather the information, it will become logical who you should contact for different information.

For example, if we are working on a project to design a model on top of an accounting system and if I only work with the accountants; it is very likely that they will not understand where the underlying data is being stored. They will most likely only understand the frontend of the accounting system. Conversely, if I were to go to the database administrator that manages the backend of that same accounting application; it is very likely that they would not understand the business case for the data they are managing.

This is why it is very important to understand that business information and technical information about your model design project will come from different places. Once you know where to go for each set of information, we can move on to rule number two.

Rule 2 – learn to dance

While working with the two different sides of the project, it is important to remember that they will often not understand each other. It is your job to be the liaison between them. The business side (in our case, the accountants) is not likely to understand the underlying table structure or the ways in which their data is being stored. In the same vein, the technical side (in our case, the database administrator) is not likely to understand the business case for how to display the data to an end user. Your job is to understand both sides and to gather the information that you need from each in order to design your model. This can be a balancing act or a dance between the two sides.

So, how do you dance? The first step is to make sure both sides are aware of the end goal of the project. In our example, the end goal is to develop a reporting system for the accountants. Many people would then assume that the accountants are the only customers for this model. In reality, that may not be the case, and they will definitely not be the only stakeholders. For the reporting system to work, the database administrator is going to have to maintain the data in a certain way. If at some point in the future they want or need to change databases, they will need to understand and mitigate the effects on this new reporting system. Also, in addition to the accountants that will be using this new model for creating ad hoc reports, there may be additional end users that are interested in the data. The upper-level management may decide at some point in the future that they would like to use this same model to put together financial reports. Sales may want to be able to report off of this in order to know when to pay commissions. Marketing may want to use parts of the information to tie back to campaign effectiveness. So, what is the goal of the project then?

One could argue that it is to meet the needs of the immediate customer (the accountants) while also creating a model that is flexible enough that it could be used by future groups as well. By stating this goal early, you can avoid potential conflict when you are asking the database administrator where information is that may not relate to the current project. Or if you are asking the accountants to help you understand what additional information might be relevant outside of their group.

Rule 3 – take baby steps

When working on a large project, it is easy to think that it makes the most sense to design your entire model at once, build the entire model at once, then publish the model and test. In reality, there are so many variables at play that at any point in the process you could run into a road block that would scrap all of your previous work. That is why it is best to take baby steps.

1. Start by identifying a handful of data items that will be needed from one table.
2. Create a connection to that one table and test your connection.
3. Publish a package with just that information and test it to see how it is formatted and how quickly it comes back.
4. Assuming that there are no performance issues, move on to connecting a second table and joining the two together and testing again.

By taking baby steps with the project, you can identify potential issues early and reduce repetitive work.

Rule 4 – know your audience

This rule was alluded to earlier, but it cannot be emphasized enough. If you understand who is going to be using your package once it is published, you can understand and anticipate some of their needs. For instance, if you are building your package for the accountants as mentioned previously, they are going to want to eventually see reports about things such as passed due accounts, aging receivables, accounts payable, and accounts that need updated contact information. By anticipating ahead of time what information they will need, you can design an effective model that includes that information in a meaningful way.

So, how do you get to know your audience? Interview them. Set up interviews with your future end users and ask them what kind of things they are interested in reporting off of. This is going to give you your best insight into the type of reports that will eventually be built and what data needs to be included in the model.

As a warning, however, you should be careful to make it clear in these interviews that all the information requested may not be available. You will be surprised at how often end users ask for reporting on data that is either not collected or has no way of being tied together. The goal of a model designer is not to end up having a full-blown data warehouse project on your hands. It is to allow end users easier access to data by creating simple metadata on the backend.

Rule 5 – get buy-in and sign off

Before starting your actual design, you should have gathered a ton of information on the model you will be designing. There is no reason to keep this information a secret. Share it. Go back to your technical team and let them know what information is being requested and verify that they can help you access all of it. Once that is verified, go back to your end users and let them know what information you are able to include. Share with them your vision of how this will be used and what reports can be created from it. Confirm that the information you are planning to give them is the information that they need. Then, finally, get them to sign off on the end deliverable. In doing this, you set yourself up for success in your model design project before you even touch Cognos Framework Manager.

Three-tier approach to model design

When designing a model in IBM Cognos Framework Manager, the recommended approach is to use a tiered design. The most common is a three-tier design. In a three-tier design, you will include a database layer, a business layer, and a presentation layer. There is some debate within the Cognos community as to whether or not the third tier is really necessary or if it is better to combine the business layer and presentation layer into one to make it a total of a two-tier model. While this can be done and works great in most scenarios, there are reasons for creating the habit of using a three-tier approach.

One major reason for using the database view layer is that it allows you to import your table structures exactly as they exist in the underlying database. By not changing anything here, you protect yourself against potential issues in case the underlying database tables change. In the database layer, some purists will not even import relationships because of the possibility of those changing at the database level. For our purposes, I will use the metadata wizard to import our relationships.

The business view layer is where relationships are created, calculations are made, formatting is set, and snowflakes are compressed down to stars.

The presentation view layer is where the objects being used by the end users are placed into logical groupings to be presented to them.

When these three layers or views are put together, we have a well-designed, three-tier Cognos Framework Manager model.

Designing a database view of your data

In Cognos Framework Manager, the database view should be an exact replica of the underlying database. This makes the design pretty easy.

When you first start Cognos Framework Manager, you will be prompted to select either **Create a new project...**, **Open a project**, or **Create a new project using Model Design Accelerator**.

For this example, we are going to create a new project. However, here is what each option will give us:

- **Create a new project...**: This will allow you to start a new Cognos Framework Manager model from scratch

- **Open a project**: This will allow you to open an existing Cognos Framework Manager model to continue development

- **Create a new project using Model Design Accelerator**: This will allow you to create a new Cognos Framework Manager model while using Model Design Accelerator to aid in the design process

For this example, we will start from scratch by selecting **Create a new project...**.

When we create a new project, we are prompted to provide a project name and a location. For this example, we are going to name our project `Cognos 10` and save it to `C:\IBM_Cognos\FM\Cognos10.cpf`. For this example, we are not checking the **Use Dynamic Query Mode** checkbox. Dynamic Query Mode is a new capability in IBM Cognos Business Intelligence V10. It will create more efficient SQL and MDX based on the data source used. It also allows for an in-memory caching without compromising security. Refer to the following screenshot:

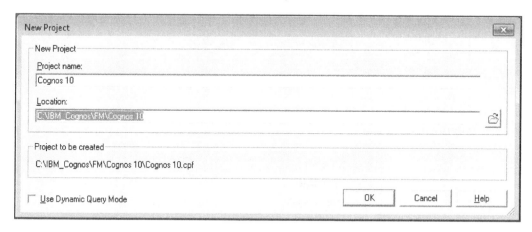

We can now select **OK**.

Now, depending on your security, you may be prompted to log in. Log in using an ID that has access to use Cognos Framework Manager.

We can now run the metadata wizard to pull in the underlying database structure for our data source. We will first create a new namespace for this metadata. A namespace is a container for metadata. The namespaces can be used to divide different groups of metadata. In our example, we are going to create three separate namespaces:

- For the database view
- For the business view
- For the presentation view

To do so, follow these steps:

1. We can start by right-clicking on the namespace named **Model**, beneath **Project**.

2. We will then go to **Create | Namespace**.

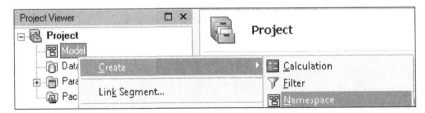

3. If we now click on the highlighted **New Namespace** namespace, we can rename it to `Database view`.

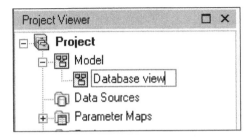

4. We will now import our database view of metadata. We can do this by right-clicking on the new namespace called **Database view** and selecting **Run Metadata Wizard...**.

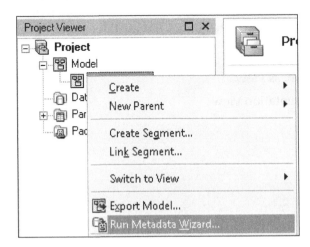

5. The first screen of the metadata wizard is **Metadata Wizard - Select Metadata Source:**

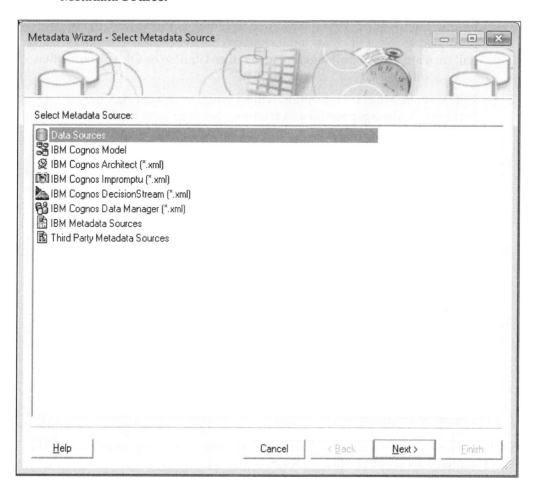

The options for metadata sources are:

- **Data Sources**: This is by far the most common metadata source. This can be any Cognos-supported data source. With this option selected, you are prompted to select or create a data source connection; the metadata wizard will then attempt to pull metadata from the database or OLAP source that is being referenced.

- **IBM Cognos Model**: This option will let you use an existing Cognos Framework Manager model as a reference for your new model.

- **IBM Cognos Architect (*.xml)**: This option allows you to use an existing IBM Cognos Architect metadata model as a source for your new Cognos Framework Manager model. Architect is a repository for metadata that was designed for sharing metadata between multiple Cognos applications. This product stopped being supported after Cognos 7.4 Maintenance Release 3.

- **IBM Cognos Impromptu (*.xml)**: This option will allow you to point to an Impromptu Catalog to import metadata.

- **IBM Cognos DecisionStream (*.xml)**: This is one of two **Extract Transact Load** (ETL) tools used within the Cognos suite of products.

- **IBM Cognos Data Manager (*.xml)**: This is the second of two ETL tools used within the Cognos suite of products.

- **IBM Metadata Sources**: This option will allow you to select from other IBM metadata sources used in tools such as InfoSphere and Rational.

- **Third Party Metadata Sources**: This option will allow you to select from a number of other metadata sources from tools outside of IBM, such as Oracle, SAP, and Sybase.

For the purpose of our example, we will use a data source to import our metadata. With **Data Sources** selected, click on **Next**.

We are now presented with a list of all existing data sources. If you have not yet set up any data sources, please move ahead to the administration section of this book to learn how to do so. For this example, we are going to use an existing data source to design our model by following these steps:

1. We will select the **gosales** data source, which is part of the IBM Cognos BI samples. Then, click on **Next**.

2. On our next screen, we are prompted to choose which objects we would like to import from our data source.

3. With this data source, we are looking at the SQL Server tables that are each in different schemas. We will import the following from the **gosl** schema: ORDER_DETAILS, ORDER_HEADER, ORDER_METHOD, PRODUCT, and PRODUCT_TYPE.

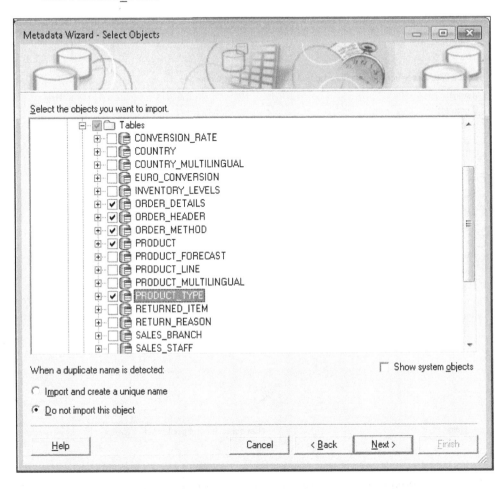

4. We can now click on **Next** to be taken to the last screen of the wizard. On this screen, we are prompted to select how to generate relationships from the underlying table structures. This screen has four main selections that have to be made. The following are the names of these sections and a brief description:

    ◦ **Select at least one criteria to detect and generate relationships**: In this section, you tell the tool how to detect relationships. The most common way is to use primary and foreign keys, which will look at the underlying tables and determine what keys are present between each.

- ° **Select between which set of objects you want to detect and generate relationships**: In this section, you can select if you want to detect relationships for the query subjects being imported only, between the imported query subjects and the existing ones, or between both. The option selected here will be determined by whether or not there are query subjects already existing in the model.

- ° **Indicate how you want to generate relationships between the imported Query Subjects**: In this section, you tell the tool how to handle outer joins (whether or not to convert them to inner joins) and whether or not to attempt to detect the granularity of a relationship.

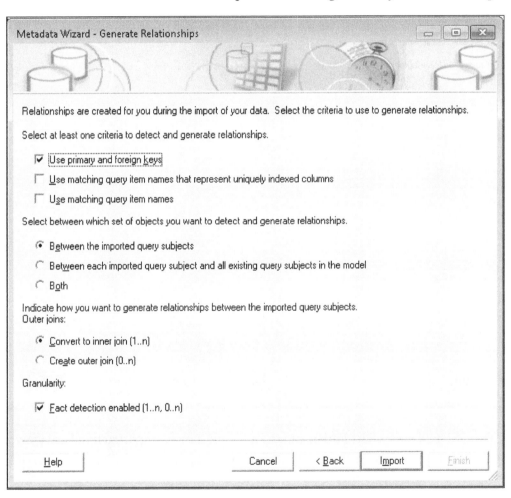

5. For our example, we will use all of the defaults and click on **Import**.

   On the final screen of the import wizard, we will be shown a summary of what was created through the import process. For this example, we have created five new query subjects and four new relationships, as shown in the following screenshot:

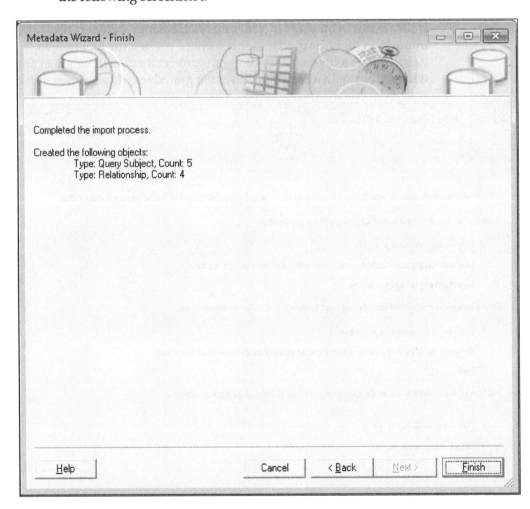

6. We will now select **Finish** and examine our newly imported database view.

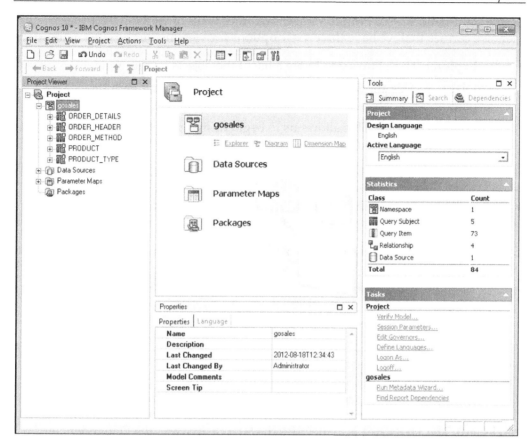

 Before we can start exploring our newly imported metadata, we should take a step back and review the different areas of Cognos Framework Manager.

The upper area of Cognos Framework Manager is the toolbar. In this area, you can perform many of the same actions that are available in the summary areas below it.

To the left of Cognos Framework Manager is **Project Viewer**. **Project Viewer** allows you to see all of the metadata that has been developed. In our current example, we can see that we have one namespace with five query subjects below it. If we expand **Data Sources**, we will also see that we have one data source (**gosales**). We have not created any Parameter Maps or Packages at this point.

To the right-hand side of **Project Viewer** are other ways of viewing the project. Here we can see that we have three view options for viewing our **gosales** namespace:

- **Explorer**: This allows you to see a list of the objects in your model
- **Diagram**: This allows us to see each query subject along with the relationships between them in a database diagram view
- **Dimension Map**: This allows us to begin designing relational OLAP dimensions from our data

Below this area is the **Properties** area. These properties will change depending on what object is selected in **Project Viewer** or the main **Project** area. Some properties will allow editing to affect how the object is formatted or if additional metadata should be added to it. Others are imported from the data and cannot be changed.

On the right-hand side of the screen, we see **Tools**. Refer to the following screenshot:

The **Tools** area includes the **Summary** page that summarizes our project and allows us to perform tasks such as reopening the metadata wizard, discovering dependencies, and editing object definitions (dynamically appears when an object is selected). The **Tools** area also includes the **Search** area and the **Dependencies** (object) viewer.

Now, returning to the middle viewer area, we have two options as to how we can view our newly imported database view. The first is the **Explorer** area that gives us an icon listing of our nine objects (five query subjects and four relationships). Refer to the following screenshot:

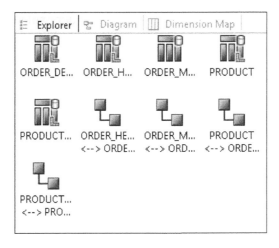

Alternatively, we can view this in the **Diagram** view, which is preferred; it shows us the different relationships between the various query subjects in a more visual and meaningful way.

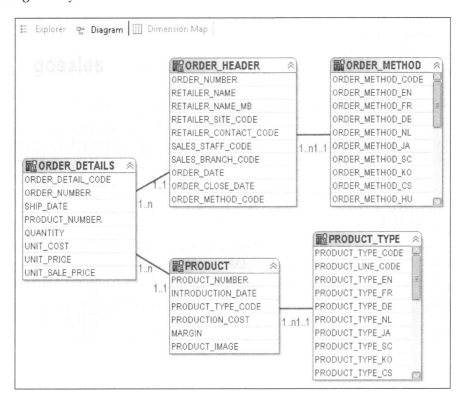

In the diagram, we can see that the ORDER_DETAILS query subject is our primary fact table, with the PRODUCT and ORDER_HEADER query subjects as the first limb dimension tables and the PRODUCT_TYPE and ORDER_METHOD query subjects as the second limb dimension tables. What I mean by this is that the information in PRODUCT relates directly to ORDER_DETAILS, whereas the information in PRODUCT_TYPE relates to PRODUCT directly but relates to the ORDER_DETAILS query subject indirectly.

Now that we have reviewed our imported database view, we need to prepare to create our physical view by better organizing our model. Follow these steps:

1. We will start by renaming our base namespace from **gosales** to **Product Orders** by clicking on the namespace twice so the name highlights and typing in the new name.

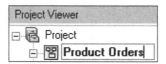

2. We will now right-click on the newly renamed namespace and go to **Create | Namespace**.

3. Name your new namespace as **Database View**. Next, while simultaneously pressing *Shift*, click on ORDER_DETAILS and PRODUCT_TYPE to select all five query subjects.

4. Then click-and-drag those over the new namespace until it highlights. Once the name of the new namespace **Database View** is highlighted, release and you will have moved all of the database query subjects into the **Database View** namespace.

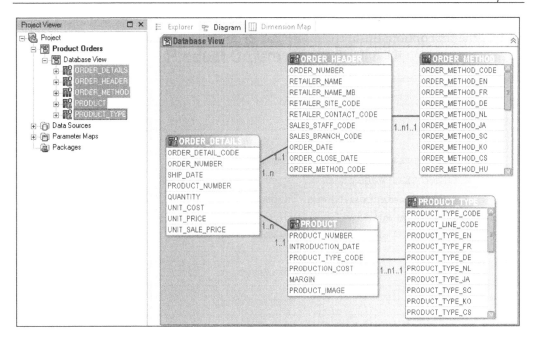

We have now completed creating our database view of metadata.

Designing a business view of your data

In our business view layer, we will look to define additional relationships if needed, create calculated items, format our data, rename the database objects to logical names, and compress our snowflake design down to a simple star design. To do so, follow these steps:

1. We will start by creating a new namespace to hold the **Business View** namespace.

2. We will again right-click on the base **Product Orders** namespace and go to **Create | Namespace**. We will name this namespace Business View.

    We will next look at consolidating our query subjects in order to have a star design with only one level from the fact table. We want to start by creating our fact table from the data available in our underlying table, ORDER_DETAILS.

3. To create a new query subject under your newly created **Business View** namespace, right-click on **Business View** and go to **Create | Query Subject**.

4. We're going to name this new query subject Order Details and choose the first option, **Build the query based on the data that exists in the model**, as shown in the following screenshot:

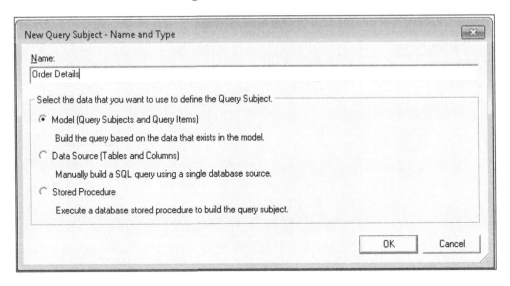

5. Click on **OK**.

6. On the next screen, expand **Database View** and ORDER_DETAILS and drag in all of the query items from under **ORDER_DETAILS**. Then click on **OK**.

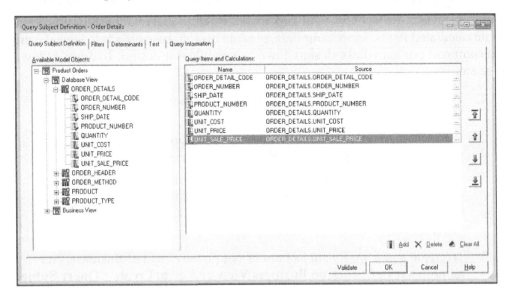

We will now proceed to create a consolidated query subject to hold information from both the PRODUCT and PRODUCT_TYPE query subjects.

7. Again, right-click on **Business View** and go to **Create | Query Subject**. This time, we will name our query subject as Product and keep the option to build based on existing data in the model, as shown in the following screenshot:

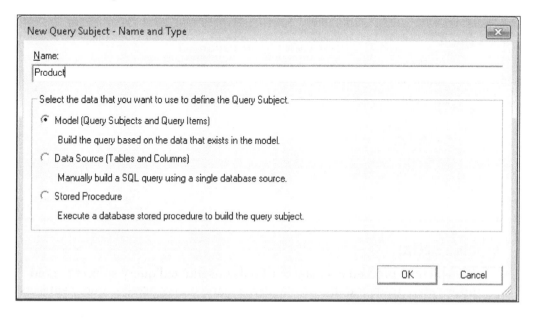

8. On the next screen, we will drag in all of the query items from PRODUCT and the first three query items from PRODUCT_TYPE.

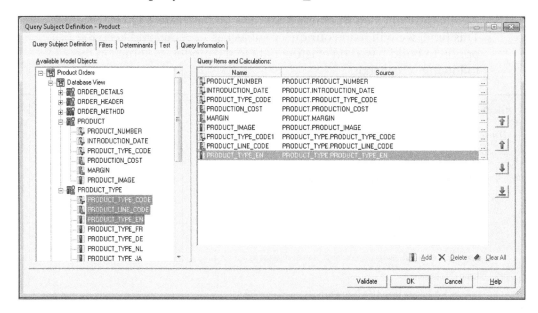

9. Click on **OK**.

    We will now proceed to create our final consolidated query subject to hold information from both the ORDER_HEADER and ORDER_METHOD query subjects.

10. Again, right-click on **Business View** and go to **Create | Query Subject**. This time, we will name our query subject as Order Header and select the **Model (Query Subjects and Query Items)** option to build our query subject based on the existing data in the model, as shown in the following screenshot:

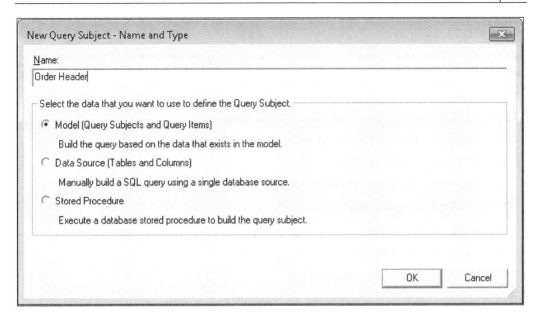

11. On the next screen, we will drag in all of the query items from ORDER_HEADER and the first two query items from ORDER_METHOD.

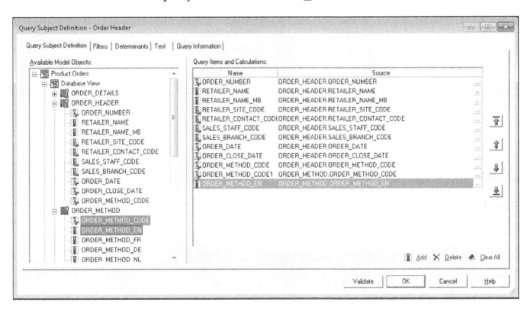

12. Click on **OK**.

We have now consolidated our query subjects down to what can be seen as a star schema. Next, we will rename the query items to logical names instead of database names. We will start in our **Order Details** query subject. We can go through query item by query item, clicking each twice to rename them. We will make the following changes:

- `ORDER_DETAIL_CODE` to **Order Detail Code**
- `ORDER_NUMBER` to **Order Number**
- `SHIP_DATE` to **Ship Date**
- `PRODUCT_NUMBER` to **Product Number**
- `QUANTITY` to **Quantity**
- `UNIT_COST` to **Cost**
- `UNIT_PRICE` to **Price**
- `UNIT_SALE_PRICE` to **Sale Price**

The following is the screenshot of the **Business View** namespace:

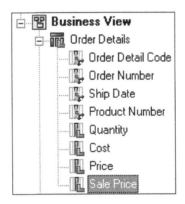

We will not proceed to change the remaining names in **Product** and **Order Header**.

For the **Product** query subject, we'll make the following changes:

- `PRODUCT_NUMBER` to **Product Number**
- `INTRODUCTION_DATE` to **Intro Date**
- `PRODUCT_TYPE_CODE` to **Product Type Code**
- `PRODUCTION_COST` to **Production Cost**
- `MARGIN` to **Margin**
- `PRODUCT_IMAGE` to **Image**

- `PRODUCT_TYPE_CODE1` is a repeat of `PRODUCT_TYPE_CODE`; delete it
- `PRODUCT_LINE_CODE` to **Product Line Code**
- `PRODUCT_TYPE_EN` to **Product Type**

For the **Order Header** query subject, we'll make the following changes:

- `ORDER_NUMBER` to **Order Number**
- `RETAILER_NAME` to **Retailer Name**
- `RETAILER_NAME_MB`, `RETAILER_SITE_CODE`, and `RETAILER_CONTACT_CODE` do not need to change; delete them
- `SALES_STAFF_CODE` to **Sales Person**
- `SALES_BRANCH_CODE` to **Branch**
- `ORDER_DATE` to **Order Date**
- `ORDER_CLOSE_DATE` to **Order Close Date**
- `ORDER_METHOD_CODE` to **Order Method Code**
- `ORDER_METHOD_CODE1` is a repeat of `ORDER_METHOD_CODE`; delete it
- `ORDER_METHOD_EN` to **Order Method**

The following is the screenshot of the **Business View** namespace:

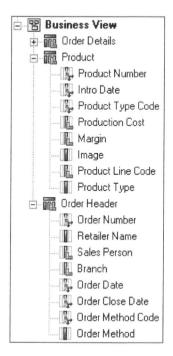

We will now go through each of our query subjects and update the formatting. The first method we will use is updating the Usage property for any items that were imported with incorrect usage. There are three types of Usage:

- Identifier: This Usage type is for query items that are used to point to a specific row of data in another table. These are almost always unique or primary keys for those tables. An example would be an order number that is unique to a specific order. It is used to identify what order is being referenced.

- Fact: This Usage type is for query items that are used as measures or can be aggregated. An example of this would be a query item for the quantity sold. This can be aggregated to multiple dimensions.

- Attribute: This Usage type is for query items that describe other query items. These do not have to always go hand in hand with an identifier, but they typically do. An example of this would be a product name. A product name is an attribute of a product number.

Each of these Usage types also has a corresponding query item icon, as shown here:

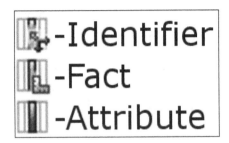

In our first query subject, **Order Details**, all of our usage seems to have imported correctly. In our second query subject, **Product**, it looks like Cognos Framework Manager has mistakenly set the **Usage** option of **Product Line Code** to **Fact**. In reality, it should be set to **Identifier**. To change this, we will select the query item in **Project Viewer** and in the drop-down under **Properties**, beside **Usage**, we will select **Identifier** as shown in the following screenshot:

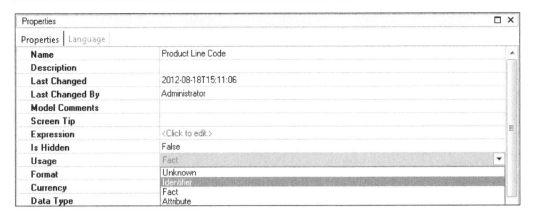

Under the **Order Header** namespace, we see that **Sales Person** and **Branch** have the same issue and need to be changed as well. We can change those now by following these steps:

1. The last thing that we will do in terms of updating **Properties** is to go through each of our facts and set a default format. Here we can look at a shortcut for setting these in bulk. We are going to select the query items from **Order Details**, such as **Cost**, **Price**, and **Sale Price**, by clicking on each while keeping *Ctrl* pressed.

2. We will also select the query items from **Product**, such as **Production Cost** and **Margin**.

 Note that now each of our query items will be listed in the **Properties** area with all properties showing as columns.

3. Scroll to the right-hand side until you see the column for **Format** and click where it says **<Click to edit.>** on the first item.

4. Within the **Data Format** pop-up window, select **Currency** from the drop-down for **Format Type** and click on **OK**.

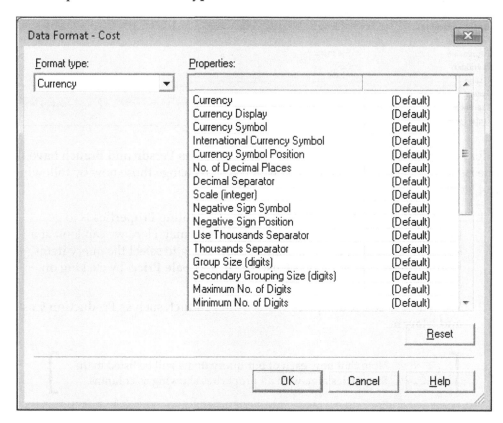

Now, notice the black downward-pointing arrow that appears beneath the highlighted **<Click to edit.>** area.

5. Click-and-drag all the five highlighted query items. This will copy the currency formatting that we just set to all items.

6. You will then receive a pop-up confirming that the properties have all been successfully updated. Click on **OK**.

We can now update **Quantity** from the **Order Details** query subject in the same way.

7. Click on **Quantity**. Next, scroll down in the **Properties** area until you find **Format** and click where it says **<Click to edit.>** in order to open the formatting pop-up.

8. Select **Number** as **Format type:** and click on **OK** as shown in the following screenshot:

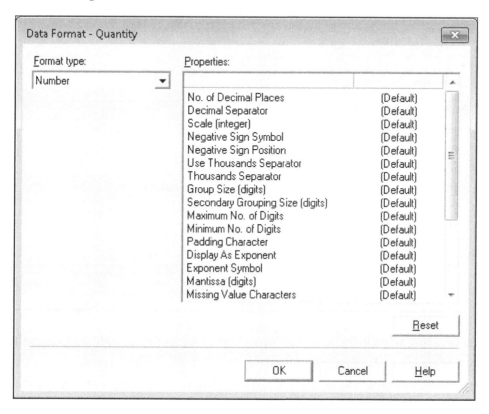

We have now completed the design of our business view layer.

Designing an end user view of your data

Designing an end user view should be the easiest step of the modeling process. By this point, we have already defined all relationships, usage, and formatting of the underlying data. Now, we just have to decide how best to present it to the end users. For our example, we will be best served if we provide two simple query subjects. One will include order information and the other will include product information.

To start things off, we will once again create a new namespace under **Product Orders**. This time we will name it Presentation View.

With our new namespace created, right-click on **Presentation View** and go to **Create | Query Subject**. We will name this first query subject Order Information and then choose the option to be imported from the model.

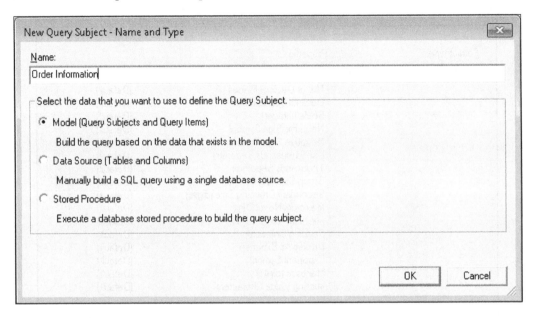

When deciding what to include, it is important to remember to only add items that may be useful to your end users. To do so, follow these steps:

1. From **Business View**, we will drag in all items from **Order Header**; and from **Order Details**, we will drag **Ship Date**, **Quantity**, **Cost**, **Price**, and **Sale Price** as shown in the following screenshot:

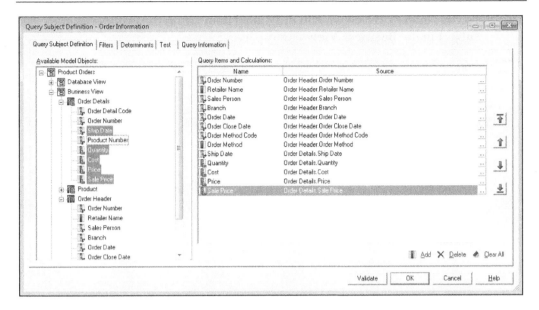

2. Click on **OK**. We will now create a new query subject for **Product Information** as well.

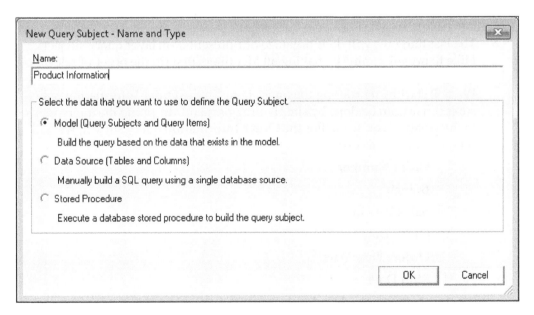

3. For this query subject, we will drag in all items from the **Product** query subject in the **Business View** namespace.

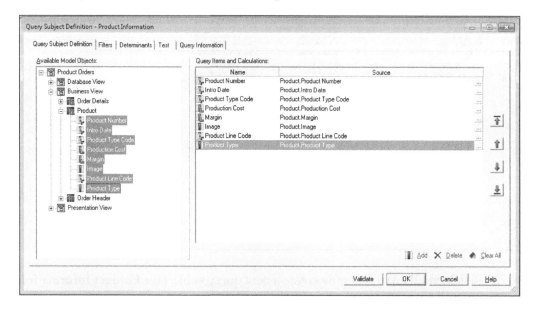

4. Click on **OK**.

5. The last thing we will do is organize our presentation layer query subjects. I like to organize mine by having all identifiers first (in the order of relevance), then the attributes, and finally all measure in a query item folder together. We will start by reordering the query items in the **Order Information** query subject. This can be done by simply dragging-and-dropping the query items to the position you want. For the **Order Information** query subject, we will set the items in this order:

   ○ **Order Number**

   ○ **Branch**

   ○ **Sales Person**

   ○ **Order Date**

   ○ **Order Close Date**

   ○ **Ship Date**

   ○ **Order Method Code**

   ○ **Order Method**

   ○ **Retailer Name**

- ° **Quantity**
- ° **Cost**
- ° **Price**
- ° **Sale Price**

6. We will now right-click on **Order Information** and go to **Create | Query Item Folder**.

7. We will name the new **Folder** query item `Measures` and drag in **Quantity**, **Cost**, **Price**, and **Sale Price** as shown in the following screenshot:

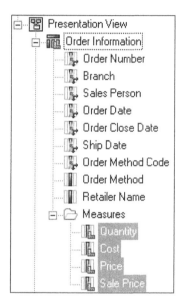

Next, we will reorder the **Product Information** query subject and organize **Product Cost** and **Margin** into the `Measures` folder as well. We will order this query subject as follows:

- **Product Number**
- **Product Line Code**
- **Intro Date**
- **Product Type Code**
- **Product Type**
- **Image**
- **Measures**

- **Production Cost**
- **Margin**

The following screenshot shows the order of query subjects:

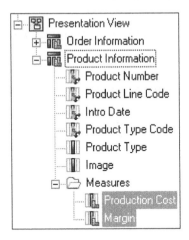

We have now completed the design of our presentation view layer.

Publishing a package

All that is left to do is publishing our package for the end users to see. Publishing a package is very simple. To do so, follow these steps:

1. We will right-click on **Packages** in **Project Viewer** and go to **Create | Package**.

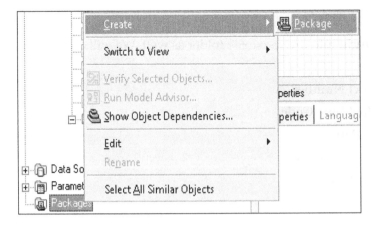

2. We will now name our package with the name we want our end users to be able to find it by. For our package, we will choose the name `Product Orders` and select **Next**. The next window will ask us what we want to publish.

3. We are going to choose to only publish **Presentation View**. Click on **Database View** and **Business View** until they have red "X" marks beside them as shown in the following screenshot:

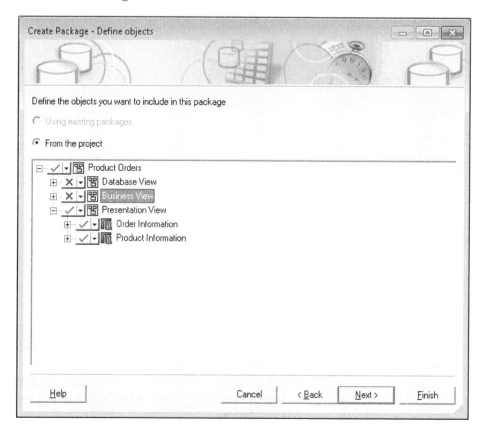

4. Click on **Next**.

5. On our next screen, we are prompted for what the underlying database is, so that Cognos can include function sets for it. Keep only the database type that you are using. In our example, we are using SQLServer.

6. Click on **Finish**.

7. Once you have created your package, you will see a window confirming the creation of it and asking if you want to open **Publish Wizard**. Publishing is what gets our newly created package in front of the end user, so select **Yes**.

8. The first screen of **Publish Wizard** will ask you where you want to publish. Best practice is to create a secured folder to hold all packages, but for the sake of ease we will move forward with the default location of **Public Folders**. Then, click on **Next** as shown in the following screenshot:

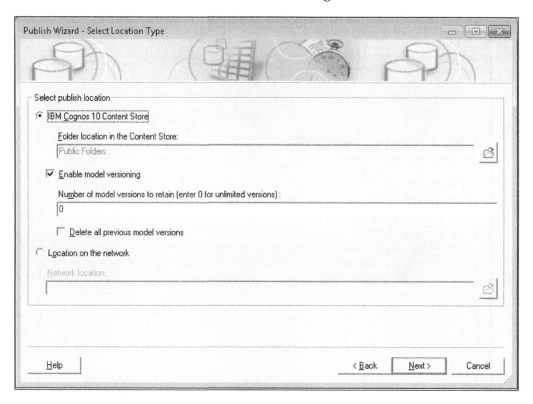

On the next screen, you will be asked if you want to add security. In some environments, it is important to set security before a package is published, instead of setting it after it is published.

9. For our example, we will just choose **Next**; in a live environment, consider setting security if you are publishing a package with sensitive information.

10. On our last screen, we are asked if we want to generate the files for externalized query subjects, if we want to verify the model before publishing, and if we want to use Dynamic Query Mode. Keep the defaults and select **Publish**.

You have now published your first model!

The business case for Cognos Framework Manager

Cognos Framework Manager is a necessary step in separating the end user from the data. Most end users are not going to be technically savvy enough to understand the underlying database structures that contain the information that they need. For that reason, it is important to have a layer between the database and the end user. That layer is designed by Cognos Framework Manager.

Understanding the problem

End users want information presented in a meaningful way. However, the data that is stored in most databases is not presented in a meaningful way. The column names rarely represent the business name of the data. In a database, the business information "Product" may be represented as PROD_NAME. However, end users want to see "Product". Another common problem is that information that may all be presented in one shared screen in an application is often stored in multiple, non-joined tables on the underlying system. The end users want to see this information presented in business terms, with all data relating to all other data. This is where Cognos Framework Manager comes in.

Understanding the solution

With Cognos Framework Manager, you can bring in the database view of data and transform it into something meaningful using metadata. This is the real power of modeling data before presenting it to end users. The other value in this is that developers within Cognos Connection are not required to recreate common calculations if they are created once at the metadata layer. This allows the developers of the metadata to control what data is presented with filters, security, and calculations. The end result should be an error-proof reporting engine for your business.

Summary

In conclusion, we have reviewed IBM Cognos Framework Manager and how to use this robust tool to build a basic metadata model. We have looked at best practices for designing that model using a multitier approach, and we have walked through basic examples of what actions are performed at each level in the model. We have also looked at how to publish an existing model for end user consumption, and what the business case is for having a metadata modeling tool such as Cognos Framework Manager.

In the next chapter, we will look at administering and performance-tuning our Cognos BI environment.

10
Administration and Performance Tuning

This chapter will help us better understand the role and function of an administrator as well as show us how to use the **Status** tab of IBM Cognos BI to performance tune our Cognos BI environment. We will also look at basic performance-tuning rules of thumb. In this chapter, we will cover:

- Deciding who should be an administrator
- Navigating the administration interface
- Monitoring the system in the **Status** tab
- Performance tuning the system
- Designing your security model
- Adding data source connections
- Importing and exporting content
- Routing your requests using routing sets
- The business case for performance tuning
- The business case for administration

Deciding who should be an administrator

Administrators need to be technical. For a new Cognos BI environment, you should look at selecting administrators that are very technical and can manage a large-scale enterprise application. In addition, administrators need to be able to understand the needs of the business. Typically, in smaller Cognos BI environments, you will see the administrator wearing multiple hats, namely designing models and reports as well as gathering requirements. In these types of scenarios, the same administrator may be setting security one minute, and the next minute could be gathering reporting requirements from a business user. Every environment should have at least one Cognos administrator that has experience being a Cognos administrator. If not, you should seek support from IBM or an IBM Business Partner to train an administrator from your internal staff.

Ultimately, anyone with a strong technical background and the ability to understand business needs could be trained to be an administrator.

Navigating the administration interface

The Cognos administration interface is integrated into Cognos Connection and can be accessed in two ways—similar to how each studio can be accessed in two ways. The first option is to choose **Administer IBM Cognos content** from the **Welcome** page as shown in the following screenshot:

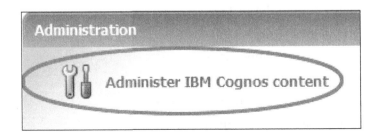

The second option is to select **IBM Cognos Administration** from the bottom of the **Launch** menu as shown in the following screenshot:

Both of these options will take you to the IBM Cognos administration interface where you can begin managing and administering the various aspects of Cognos BI.

You will notice inside the **IBM Cognos Administration** area that the environment is organized by tabs in the same way that that the end user interface of Cognos Connection is organized. The first three tabs are the primary tabs for managing your Cognos BI environment. They are **Status**, **Security**, and **Configuration**, and they each can be used for different key elements of administration as shown in the following screenshot:

The description of these three tabs is as follows:

- **Status**: This tab allows you to monitor activities, processes, and schedules in your Cognos BI environment.
- **Security**: This tab allows you to define security groups and roles, map security profiles to capabilities within Cognos BI, and manage user interface profiles.
- **Configuration**: This tab allows you to set up data sources, distributions, printers, and portlets. It also allows you to manage content deployments and styles. Finally, it allows you to configure each of the various services and processes running in your Cognos BI environment.

Monitoring the system in the Status tab

If you select the **Status** tab, you will notice that there are a few sections within it. The first three sections (**Current Activities**, **Past Activities**, and **Upcoming Activities**) are all related to activities running on the system. These are great for understanding what your users are actively, or through scheduling, running on the system. The final option allows you to see all the reports with the schedules. If you are setting up your environment, this will allow you to identify any peaks in usage that could potentially hurt performance. For the purpose of monitoring, we are going to focus on the **System** section. When you select **System**, you will notice that the monitoring screen provided is set up like a Metric Studio scoreboard:

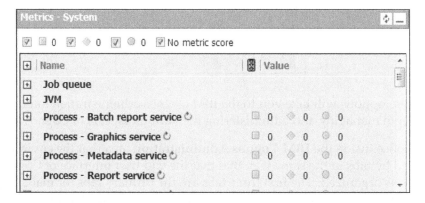

For the purpose of this book, let's assume that we have not yet set the values that we want to strive for. To be honest, it takes time to understand what you should set each of those values to, for your environment. Once you have tweaked your system for a few weeks or months, you will begin to understand what values to strive for within each of these metrics. When you are ready to set your metrics, you can click on the + button to the right-hand side of the process that you would like to set up. Then set your high and low watermarks by choosing the pencil icon at the side of each option. This will begin to give you a picture of how your metrics look. The services that are most important to the performance of your system are:

- **Report service**: This service manages interactive requests to have reports run, and it provides live, interactive output. This is used for live report runs either from Cognos Connection or from within one of the various studios in Cognos BI.

- **Batch report service**: This service manages behind-the-scenes requests to have reports run. These are typically scheduled requests that will run on the backend. It also provides the output to be stored in the content store and saved for interactive viewing.

- **Content manager service**: This service talks to and writes back to the content store. This is the service that will add a new record to the content store database when activities are performed. Also, it is used during deployments from within Cognos BI.

- **Report data service**: This service is very important if you implement a mobile reporting solution, as it manages the transfer of the data from your Cognos BI environment to the mobile platform. Since you typically have executives running and utilizing mobile BI, you want to make sure that this is tuned appropriately so that reports are delivered quickly to mobile devices.

Performance tuning the system

The real goal of monitoring is so that you can understand what good performance metrics are and begin to tune your system to hit those. One of the biggest roles of a Cognos administrator is keeping the environment running, and running quickly. This can be a challenge for a number of reasons. Some of the most common causes of performance issues are there not being enough RAM, there not being enough CPUs, a misconfigured environment, too many users, too large a Cognos Content Store, and many more. So the challenge when you encounter performance issues is determining what is causing those issues. Natively in Cognos BI, this leads to a game of trial and error. For the sake of those of you who are about to start this game, we will provide an overview of how best to performance tune. Remember that each environment will be different and that there is no magic configuration that will work with all environments. This is by no means an all-encompassing guide to performance tuning, but these are some of the most common things that administrators will see.

A good place to start is to adjust your memory usage configuration in **IBM Cognos Configuration**. By default, this will be set to **768** MB. Depending on your server platform, you may want to adjust this upwards or downwards. For instance, if you are using a Windows operating system with multiple dispatchers on the same server, it is recommended that you tune this down to 512 MB. If your machine has enough RAM to handle more, you can then begin tuning this up to see when performance begins to be impacted. In general, you probably do not want to go below 512 MB or over 1536 MB.

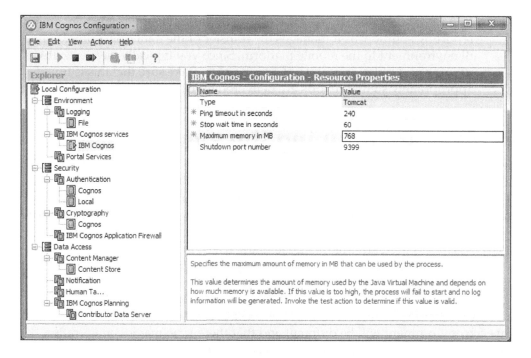

For Linux or Unix environments, you can likely leave this to be the same or even tune this up to 1024 MB to see if it improves performance. Keep in mind that the higher you set this, the longer that garbage collection will take once the process is no longer in use by Cognos BI.

I would like to share a few tips for keeping Cognos BI performing well. The first relates to setting the maximum number of processes that different services can use. The two main services that actually take up a high-memory process are **Batch report service** and **Report service**. Between these two processes, you want to have your total maximum number of processes equal to the number of threads available from your machine minus one. So if you have a basic system with two quad-core CPUs, you would have eight total threads available. In this scenario, you would want to limit your maximum processes to seven.

When setting the maxes for these, it is important to understand how your environment is most often used. If most of the reports in your environment are scheduled, then you would want to lean more heavily toward **Batch report service** and less toward **Report service**. With the earlier configuration, you may want to set the maxes to five and two respectively, or four and three if you think it is more evenly balanced.

With regards to RAM, it depends on the type of Cognos BI server you are running. If you are running a 32-bit Cognos Business Intelligence Server, it is recommended that you have 1.5 GB of RAM for each core, that is, up to 1 GB of RAM for the `Java.exe` file that runs with Cognos BI and 2 GB of RAM for your operating system. So with the eight core machines referenced earlier, you would need at least 15 GB of RAM. If you are running on a 64-bit machine with a 64-bit Cognos Business Intelligence Server installed, you will need to increase to 2 GB of RAM for each core. With the same example, you would need at least 19 GB of RAM. These are only estimates, and it is best to contact IBM for a complete sizing discussion that will incorporate user counts, types of reports, peak periods, and many other variables.

Designing your security model

Understanding how Cognos BI security works and setting up the proper security is essential in any reporting environment for information that needs to be protected. The need to protect data can be based on how sensitive the data is to your stakeholders, or it could be governed by laws and regulations such as we see with healthcare and financial information. To understand how Cognos BI security all ties together, we will start by looking at an overview of the various pieces of Cognos BI security.

The CAF

The **Cognos Application Firewall (CAF)** can be turned on inside of Cognos Configuration. You simply set **Enable CAF validation?** to **True** and restart your environment:

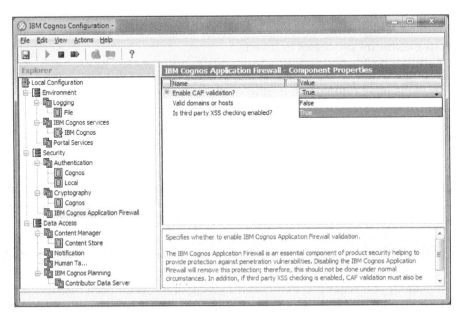

The CAF will protect your environment from outside attacks. It is a very good idea to leave the CAF turned on with outward-facing environments that are not secured heavily by other means.

The only major drawback of the CAF being turned on is that it limits use by external applications to Cognos BI. Because the CAF does not recognize applications as safe and approved, what happens is that each computer that wants to connect to Cognos BI using an external application would need to be set up as a valid domain or host in Cognos Configuration. In addition, CAF only applies to the gateway and it can be bypassed by pointing directly to a dispatcher.

External security

External security can be whatever security provider you use to maintain security within your environment. It is considered external because it is not the standard Cognos BI security that comes within Cognos BI. Most environments choose to add their Active Directory or LDAP security to Cognos BI in order to make authentication and maintenance easier. Typical external security options are Active Directory, LDAP, custom Java providers, SiteMinder, and SAP.

When you utilize an external security and set it up as a Cognos BI namespace, you are allowing Cognos BI to read from that security provider and confirm if a user is authenticated to that security provider. Then, you can use the other aspects in Cognos BI security to identify what that authenticated user is able to do within Cognos BI.

Cognos BI security

So that brings us to Cognos BI security. When Cognos BI is installed, there is a security setup that has roles defined within the Cognos namespace. A role is a collection of authenticated users that can all be secured together. Predefined Cognos BI roles are set up based on the capabilities within Cognos BI. An example of a role is **Query users**. This role is then added to the permissions for the capability to use Query Studio. With this scenario, any user added to **Query users** would then have access to Query Studio and vice versa. You can also create groups here. Many administrators struggle with the difference between a group and a role as these are distinct options within Cognos BI.

A group is detailed by the icon of two people standing together:

A group should be used to combine people that should have access to the same sets of data. You may have a group that is called Human Resources and add members of the Human Resources team to it, then secure your Human Resources data so that only that group has access to it.

A role is detailed by the icon of two people standing together with hats on, as shown in the following screenshot:

It is hard to believe that anyone would get these two confused, right?

A role should be used to combine people that should have the same Cognos BI capabilities. Think of this as their role within the Cognos BI environment. So, you can have roles called Report Developers for people that will be developing reports.

In some environments, you see groups and roles combined. In a scenario like this, you might see a group or role called Human Resources Report Developers. In such a role, you would only have those report developers that should have access to Human Resources data. While this is widely used, it is not the best practice and can lead to confusion while securing an environment.

Capabilities

Capabilities allow users to do things within Cognos BI. Capabilities can be set for accessing areas both at high levels (access to Report Studio) and low levels (being able to define your own SQL in Report Studio). Essentially, capabilities define who can do what within Cognos BI.

How it all works together

Using the descriptions given later, let's walk through how to set up security effectively. You must first decide if you want to keep the Cognos BI native security turned on. The advantage of the Cognos BI native security is that you as an administrator can create your own groups and roles within Cognos BI and map the external groups to them. This gives you more flexibility to manage access rights.

The next decision is whether or not you want to use external security. It is highly recommended that you do utilize this since your organization is likely to already have some type of security in place that would be supported.

Now you have to consider how to model your security. For modeling your security, you must consider two key questions:

* What do you want people to be able to do?
* What do you want people to be able to see?

What people can do

We secure what people can do using the capabilities part of Cognos BI. Depending on the size of your organization, you may not want to manually add each individual user to a capability. So what is typically done is that, within Cognos BI security, roles are set up that are based on functional capabilities. You may utilize the existing roles that do an adequate job of defining Cognos BI access rights, or you can create your own.

What people can see

To secure what people can see, you must go to each individual item in your environment and set the security. Imagine doing this for each user as well; it would become an administration nightmare. This is why groups and roles are utilized. In addition to this, you can set objects to inherit security from the objects above them in the folder structure of Cognos Connection, and this limits the need to secure every single object. To set the security on an object, you are given a few options. Let's see how to secure the **GO Sales and Retailers** package so that only Report Administrators have access to the package. To do so, follow these steps:

1. First, we will select the **Set properties - GO Sales and Retailers** icon to the right of the **GO Sales and Retailers** package as shown in the following screenshot:

2. In the properties menu, go to the **Permissions** tab. You will notice that there is a default security already set for this object.

3. Select the **Override the access permissions acquired from the parent entry** option. Then, select all items by selecting the check mark in the upper-left corner of your permissions list as shown in the following screenshot:

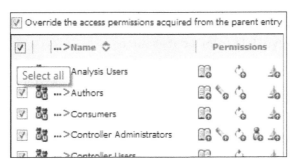

4. At the bottom of the inherited permissions list, click on **Remove** to clear all of the selected permissions. The **Permissions** area should now say **No entries**.

5. Select the **Add...** option to add the report administrators.

6. Next, select the **Cognos** namespace. Find **Report Administrators** in the list and select the checkbox beside that role.

7. While selected, you can click on the green add arrow to move the role into the **Selected entries** area:

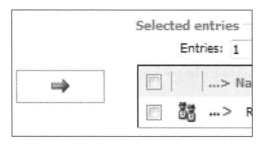

8. Click on **OK**.

9. Select the checkbox beside the newly added role, and to the right-hand side note that you have the ability to update the permissions to either grant access or deny access.

   The permissions available are:

   ° **Read**: This will allow the user, group, or role to read all properties of an object or create a shortcut to an object.

   ° **Write**: This will allow the user, group, or role to modify or create new objects within a location or edit an existing object. This option essentially allows users to update.

   ° **Execute**: This will allow the user, group, or role to run a report or retrieve data from a data source.

   ° **Set Policy**: This will allow the user, group, or role to update the security permissions for an object, as we are doing in this section now for **Go Sales and Retailers**.

   ° **Traverse**: This will allow the user, group, or role to view what is inside a folder or package without having additional access to it. With this permission, you can see basic properties of the object, such as its name and description.

10. Grant all and select **OK** to complete the security change.

Adding data source connections

After the installation, the first thing that you will need to do, in order to take advantage of your new Cognos BI environment, is to add a data source. A data source is a connection used to connect a set of data. In this case, it is a connection to connect data that you want to use for building reports. Cognos BI can connect to virtually any data source. There are native connections available for most major data source types, including but not limited to, DB2, SQL Server, Oracle, Neteeza, and so on. In addition to this, you can create ODBC data source connections to any data source that is supported through ODBC, and you can connect to nontraditional data sources through a tool that is delivered free of charge with Cognos BI called IBM Virtual View Manager. With the addition of Dynamic Query Mode, it is best practice to use JDBC drivers to connect to data sources so that Dynamic Query Mode can be fully utilized.

Let's walk through creating a data source connection from scratch. You will first need to navigate to the **Configuration** tab in Cognos administration page. Note that the first option will be **Data Source Connections**. To create a new data source connection, select the icon that looks like a database icon as shown in the following screenshot:

Follow these steps:

1. On the next screen, you will be asked to provide a name, description, and screen tip. Only the name is required.

2. We will name ours `Data Source Example` and leave the **Description:** and **Screen tip:** options blank. Once you have entered your data source name, click on **Next** as shown in the following screenshot:

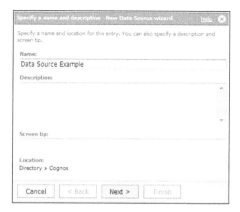

3. On the next screen, you are prompted to select your database **Type**.

   The corresponding list of database options has over 30 potential choices. These include IBM data sources, such as DB2, Informix, Neteeza, Red Brick, and Cognos cubes, as well as all of the other major database options, such as Microsoft SQL Server, Oracle, Sybase, SAP, and Teradata. Depending on the data source that you select, the next screen will be customized for entering parameters that relate to that connection type.

4. We will choose **Microsoft SQL Server (SQL 2008 Native Client)** for our example and then click on the **Next** button.

5. For SQL Server, you are required to enter information in the **Server name**, **Database name**, and **Sign on** options.

6. You can then select the **Test the connection** option at the bottom of the page; this will bring you to a page with the **Connection string** and **Dispatcher** information.

7. Click on the **Test** button to see if you have made a valid connection to your newly set up data source as shown in the following screenshot:

8. Once you have verified that your connection is valid, you can click on **Next** again at the bottom of the screen.

9. You can now choose **Finish** to complete the data source creation process.

Importing and exporting content

We can now look at adding content to our environment. Content maintenance is important for a number of reasons. In IBM Cognos BI, you can use the **Content Administration** section under the **Configuration** tab in Cognos Administration to manage this, as shown in the following screenshot:

There are only a few purposes of using the **Content Administration** option that make sense for a Cognos administrator:

- **Exporting for backup purposes**: The content in Cognos Connection can be exported periodically as a form of backing up your system. This allows complete content store recovery if your entire system were to ever become compromised.

- **Exporting for deployment purposes**: The content in Cognos Connection can also be exported for the sole purpose of moving it to another Cognos BI environment. This is often used for deploying content from a development environment to a production environment that is used by the external customers of stakeholders.

- **Importing for deployment purposes**: This is done on the new server after content that was designed to be deployed has been exported. This content has to be physically moved to a location that can be accessed from the importing server.

- **Exporting during migrations between Cognos BI versions**: This is done when you have parallel environments that you are moving content between. I do not recommend this approach to migration because creating a copy of the Content Store is a much more efficient way to move content between Cognos BI versions.

- **Importing during migrations between Cognos BI versions**: This is also done when you have parallel environments that you are moving content between. Again, I do not recommend this approach of migrating content between Cognos BI versions.

In order to begin a new export, choose the **New Export** icon at the top of the screen that looks like an arrow pointing from a database into an open box, as shown in the following screenshot:

Follow these steps:

1. On the next screen, you will be asked to provide a name, description, and screen tip. Only the name is required.

2. We will name ours Export Example and leave the **Description** and **Screen tip** options blank. Once you have your export package name entered, click on **Next** as shown in the following screenshot:

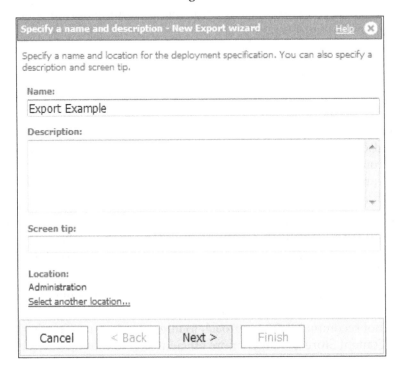

We are then given an option to select **Deployment method**. Here we can decide if we want to export by selecting either **The entire content store** or **Select public folders and directory content**.

3. We will choose **Select the entire content store** and click on **Next**.

4. We are now prompted to give the exported deployment package a deployment archive name. We will leave ours as Export Example and click on **Next** as shown in the following screenshot:

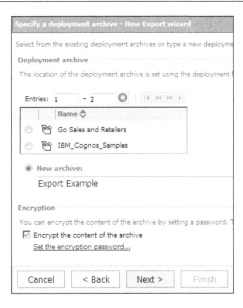

5. You will also require the **Set the encryption password...** option for your exported deployment archives.

6. When you click on **Next**, you will be shown a summary.

7. Click on **Next** again, and you will be asked to choose between the **Save and run once**, **Save and schedule**, and **Save only** options.

8. We will choose **Save and run once** and click on **Finish**. Select **Now** and then click on **Run**, as shown in the following screenshot:

So, where did that actually go? The setting for where archive packages are stored is set within the Cognos configuration. In the **Environment** section, the deployment location is set where it says **Deployment files location**, and the default location is ../deployment:

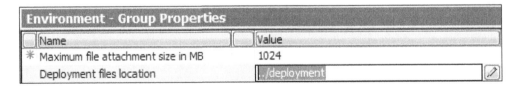

So, what does that actually mean? If we look into the installation location for Cognos BI, there will be a folder called deployment that will now have our newly created export as a ZIP file:

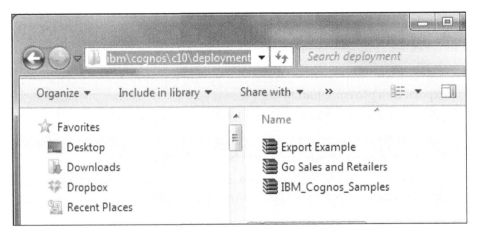

A common best practice is to redirect this archive location to a shared folder on a mapped drive that can be accessed from all of your Cognos BI environments. This will eliminate the need to physically move the export ZIP files between servers during deployments.

We will now look at the process of an import. To import, you will need to select the **New Import** icon that looks like an open box with an arrow pointing from inside of it to a database, as shown in the following screenshot:

We will be shown a list of the ZIP files that are located in the archive location that we just looked at. In our example, we have two from Cognos BI samples plus our newly created **Export Example**, as shown in the following screenshot:

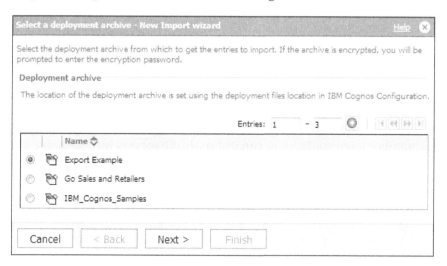

Let's carry out these steps:

1. We will select **Export Example** and then click on **Next**. We are then prompted to enter our password and click on **Next** until we get to the screen that asks us to choose between the **Save and run once**, **Save and schedule**, and **Save only** options.

2. We will choose **Save and run once** and click on **Finish**. Select **Now** and then click on **Run**. For our example, we will also need to rename the import. We will call it **Import Example** since the **Export Example** import already exists.

We have now successfully exported and imported content from Cognos BI while also understanding where it is physically stored and some best practices for minimizing efforts during deployments.

Routing your requests using routing sets

A routing set is a tool in Cognos BI that allows you to route requests to specific folders based on either the user sending the request or the package on which the request was sent. Routing sets are often used to ensure that key users and key reporting requirements have the best possible performance. Imagine if your executives have reports that they like to run periodically that run in a server-intensive way. If you put them on the same server as all of the users, they could experience performance issues, as could the other users on that same server.

Now imagine that every request from an executive is routed to a specific server, maybe a beefier, more powerful server. In this scenario, the executives have better performance and the other end users are not affected. This is the real purpose behind the use of routing sets.

Routing sets can only be used in environments with multiple dispatchers.

In order to set up routing rules, we have to perform three major steps:

1. Step one is to put each of your servers into a Server group. A Server group is a single or multiple servers that will load balance requests. You can create any name that you would like for your various groups, but you must remember them so that you can put multiple servers into the same group. We will add one of my dispatchers to **Example Group**. To do this, follow these steps:

    i.   Open the **System** section from the **Status** tab and click on the server to see the dispatcher beneath it.

    ii. We'll then choose the downward pointing arrow beside the dispatcher and select **Set properties**.

    iii. Once we are in the properties section, we can choose the **Settings** tab and then **Tuning** from the **Category** drop-down list:

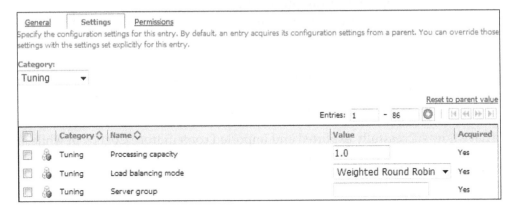

2. The second step is to set up named routing sets for users (groups or roles) and packages. To set the routing sets on a group or role, navigate to the group or role in your security area of the **Administration** area. We can work with system administrators by following these steps:

    i.   Select the **Set properties** option to the right-hand side of the **System Administrators** option in our list of roles under Cognos BI. At the bottom, we see an **Advanced routing** option. Then, click on **Edit...**:

ii. The default naming option is for **System Administrators**. So leave that and choose the green add arrow to add it to the list of sets. Then click on **OK**, and click on **OK** again.

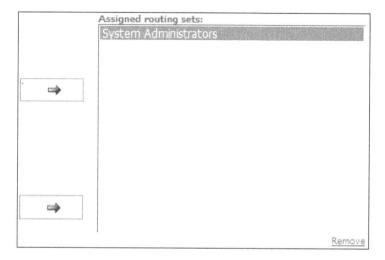

iii. We can now go back to the **Set properties** area of the **Go Sales and Retailers** package, and at the bottom you will see a similar option for the **Advanced routing** option.

iv. Check the **Overwrite the routing sets acquired from the parent entry** checkbox, and then click on the **Set...** link to define the routing sets as shown in the following screenshot:

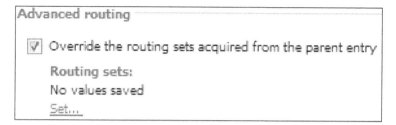

v. We can name our new set Example Package Set and add it to the sets list using the green arrow. Then click on **OK** twice.

3. Our third and final step is to set up the routing:

    i. We do this from within the **Configuration** tab in the **Dispatchers and Services** section. At the top right, there is the **Specify routing rules** option that looks like a small gear next to a server. Within here, we can set up any combination of routing options that we would like using the routing sets that we created and the server groups that have been defined. Refer to the following screenshot:

    ii. We will choose **Add a rule** twice to add one rule for routing the system administrators role and one rule for routing the **Go Sales and Retailers** requests:

We have not set up both user-role and package-based routing sets. Give this a try in a large environment to see how routing can really improve performance for key users and on key data.

The business case for performance tuning

Any Cognos BI environment will only be of value if people are using it. Too often, I have seen companies make major investments in an enterprise-level reporting environment only to see it underutilized due to poor performance. Ultimately, this can be avoided. If you are with a client, or if you are a client, that is constantly dealing with complaints about how poor the performance is in Cognos BI, there is hope. Cognos BI is not a slow running system. Cognos BI is a worldwide enterprise reporting tool that is used by some of the largest companies in the world. So, how do you change that mindset? You performance tune your environment. The executives and key stakeholders in the business want reporting and analytics. However, let's face it; they don't want to wait on it. That is why, from a business perspective, performance tuning is essential.

To put it simply, the business case for performance tuning is that the tool will not be utilized without good performance. The only way to ensure good performance is through constant monitoring and tuning of the environment, to make sure that everything is running smoothly.

The business case for administration

Administration is the glue that holds all of the pieces together. While the businesses likely does not understand all of the integrated details of what makes Cognos BI run, they are the ones that are utilizing the end results. Without administration, Cognos BI doesn't work. There would be no reports or dashboards. There would be no studios from which to design reports. Administration is crucial to all of it.

If you find yourself in a situation where you need to help justify an additional administrator to a business that may not want to spend money, talk about all of the things that have to happen in order to make sure that reports are delivered and systems run smoothly. You can use the process of setting security, adding data, and monitoring the performance of the system within your business. At the end of the day, any Cognos BI environment will only be as good as its administrator.

Summary

In this chapter, we have covered a ton of information for administrators, but there is still a ton more we can learn. We have reviewed how to select the right administrator as well as how to be administered.

From a technical perspective, we reviewed the Cognos Administration interface. We looked at performance monitoring and performance tuning using the **Status** tab in conjunction with the **Configuration** tab. We looked at how to set up security and data sources. We looked at content maintenance and the different uses for it as well as some best practices for it. We also looked at how to use advanced routing sets to improve performance and better load-balance server requests.

From a business perspective, we addressed the business cases for both performance tuning and performance administration.

In the next chapter, we will focus on the best practices for Cognos BI. We will look at some tools that are available, to make managing a Cognos BI environment easier, and we'll take a deeper look at increasing user adoption and the role that user adoption plays in a successful implementation.

11
Streamlining Common Administrator Tasks

This chapter will go into detail about the tools that my current company has developed to improve the lives of Cognos administrators, and fulfill regulatory requirements around source control within your reporting environment.

In this chapter, the tools we'll talk about are tools that every Cognos administrator I have ever spoken with wants. Each and every tool makes sense and makes Cognos BI a better product. With that said, they are not free. If you are one of the many customers out there that already have these tools in conjunction with your IBM Cognos BI installation, then congratulations. This will be a great chapter for you to better understand what you have. If you are one of the customers out there that does not yet have these tools, I encourage you to prepare yourself to be amazed by how much better it can be.

In this chapter, we will look at common Cognos administrator tasks and how they can be streamlined or automated using third-party BSP software tools. The BSP software's MetaManager has seven logical sections and over 28 modules:

- **Update**: This validates whether reports are working or not, makes bulk changes to reports, edits object information, edits prompt information, edits report specifications, and more

- **Blast**: This distributes pagelets to end users, distributes standard headers and footers to reports, updates preferences in bulk, updates sign-ons in bulk, updates schedules in bulk, and more

- **Secure**: This replicates security on objects, users, groups, or roles; edits security through a drag-and-drop interface; audits security and access permissions; migrates security between namespaces; and more

- **Deploy**: This backs up content, restores content, moves content directly between environments, extracts content from the content store, and more

- **Document**: This searches reports, documents reports, documents the environment, documents a model, pushes metadata to reports as screen tips, manages Content Store size, and more

- **Extend**: This performs bulk updates on Cognos Framework Manager models, connects cubes to Cognos BI in bulk, edits cubes in bulk, runs Cognos BI Jobs from the command line, and more

- **License Auditor**: This audits your Cognos BI license usage for free

We will also look at how you can integrate version control into your Cognos BI environment to reduce regulatory risks that arise from not maintaining proper source control over your IBM Cognos BI reporting and analytics environment. Some of the many tasks we will review include:

- Bulk updating Framework Manager models
- Validating report objects
- Bulk updating reports
- Applying screen tips to report outputs
- Managing security
- Distributing portal tabs
- Standardizing headers and footers
- Backing up, restoring, and deploying content
- Documenting content, security, and models
- Versioning content
- Archiving content outputs
- Retrieving deleted content
- The business case for add-on tools

Bulk updating Framework Manager models

Within BSP Software's MetaManager product, you have the ability to bulk update Framework Manager models. Natively in Cognos BI, when you want to make a change to a model, it can be cumbersome. Meta Editor was designed to allow for quick searching in and updating of these models. To access this module, click on the **Meta Editor** tab of the navigation area as shown in the following screenshot:

The first thing that we must do is open a Framework Manager model for editing. We can do that by selecting the open icon at the top of the screen next to where it says **Meta Editor**, as shown in the following screenshot:

For the purpose of this example, we will open `gosales_goretailers.cpf` from the Cognos BI samples.

The most powerful features of Meta Editor are the ability to search and the ability to perform mass edits. Therefore, we will review both of these abilities here.

First, we will look at the search ability. We can use either the **Quick Filter** or **Advanced Filter** option as shown in the following screenshot:

We will start by looking at the options available in **Quick Filter** as shown in the following screenshot:

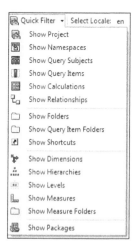

- **Show Project**: This will select the project from the model and allow it to be edited in the grid view

- **Show Namespaces**: This will select all the namespaces from the model and allow them to be edited in the grid view

- **Show Query Subjects**: This will select all the query subjects from the model and allow them to be edited in the grid view

- **Show Query Items**: This will select all the query items from the model and allow them to be edited in the grid view

- **Show Calculations**: This will select all the calculations from the model and allow them to be edited in the grid view

- **Show Relationships**: This will select all the relationships from the model and allow them to be edited in the grid view

- **Show Folders**: This will select all the folders from the model and allow them to be edited in the grid view

- **Show Shortcuts**: This will select all the shortcuts from the model and allow them to be edited in the grid view

- **Show Dimensions**: This will select all the dimensions from the model and allow their editing in the grid view

- **Show Hierarchies**: This will select all the hierarchies from the model and allow them to be edited in the grid view

- **Show Levels**: This will select all the levels from the model and allow them to be edited in the grid view

- **Show Measures**: This will select all the measures from the model and allow them to be edited in the grid view

- **Show Measure Folders**: This will select all the measure folders from the model and allow them to be edited in the grid view

- **Show Packages**: This will select all the packages from the model and allow them to be edited in the grid view

We will walk through an example using query items by following these steps:

1. We will first select **Show Query Items**.

   This will select all the query items in the model and load them into the grid. All of the available properties will now be loaded into the grid as well. The grayed out properties cannot be edited. The white properties can be edited and even edited in bulk. As an example, we can select multiple rows of the **Description** column and copy and paste these descriptions into the **Screen Tip** column. Refer to the following screenshot:

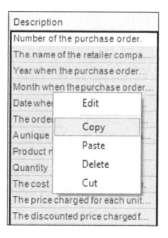

2. After copying the descriptions and highlighting the first cell under **Screen Tip**, right-click and choose **Paste** as shown in the following screenshot:

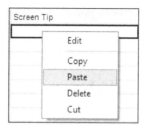

3. From within **Meta Editor**, you can also copy items from the grid out to Excel, make mass edits, and then paste them back into **Meta Editor**.

4. To save your Framework Manager model, click on the save icon at the top, as shown in the following screenshot:

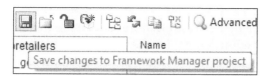

5. Next, we will look at **Advanced Filter** options. With **Advanced Filter** options, you can filter within various parts of the model. As an example, we will filter within **Query Item** where the name of the query item contains the product.

6. We will then click on **Apply** to apply the filter as shown in the following screenshot:

With this, we will bring up all the query items that contain the word product. We can then proceed to perform mass edits as needed.

Validating report objects

We will now look at validating report objects using the **Report Validator** option. It is a tool that has been designed to allow bulk validations and individual report repairs. To access the **Report Validator** option, select it from **Update | Report Validator** in the navigation section of MetaManager as shown in the following screenshot:

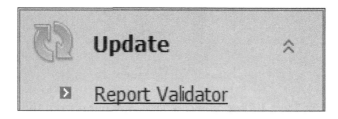

Here you can select one or multiple reports to perform individual or bulk validations. For our example, we know that a new Framework Manager model was recently published, but we do not know if it has impacted any reports. Therefore, we want to begin by validating just a few reports to see if they were affected by the model change. To do this, we must first log in to the environment where the model was published. I have already set up my environment for the purpose of this book, but if you have not, there are details on how to do so within the documentation of MetaManager.

For our example, we will assume that we have made changes to the **GO Sales and Retailers** package. Let's begin by navigating to that package's folder that contains Report Studio reports. Follow these steps:

1. We will select the first 10 reports by simultaneously pressing *Shift* and clicking on the first report **Actual Sales Against Target Sales** and tenth report **Global Sales**. This will highlight all 10 reports.

2. We will then click-and-drag the 10 reports onto the section that says **Drag items from the portal tree to this area**, as shown in the following screenshot:

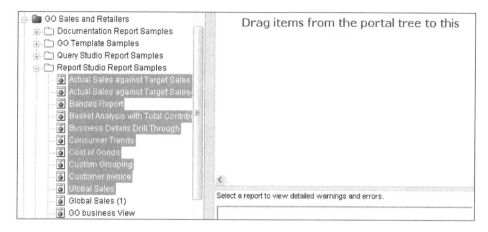

3. We can now click on the **Validate** button at the bottom to see which reports are valid and which are not.

4. With the changes that we made, we have 9 of our 10 reports showing as invalid. If we right-click on one, we can then choose **Fix Report** to bring up a dialog to update the broken reports as shown in the following screenshot:

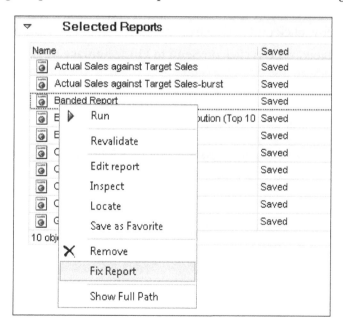

The **Fix Report** dialog will allow you to simply drag-and-drop the new query items over the broken expressions for the old ones.

5. With our example, we will drag **Product lines**, **Product types**, and **Product names** from **Products** to replace the broken corresponding expressions. As we do so, we will see the Xs turn into check marks as shown in the following screenshot:

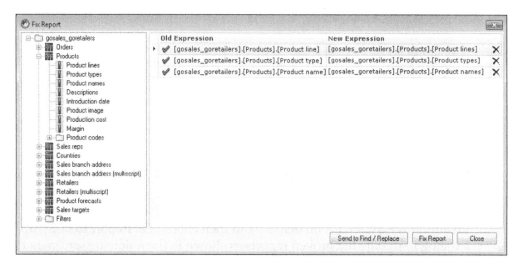

6. We can now click on **Fix Report** to apply the updates to the report.

7. Alternatively, we can click on **Send to Find/Replace** to make these changes to the **Find/Replace** module and apply them across multiple objects.

8. To complete the one-time change, we will click on **Fix Report**. On the **Report Validator** screen, right-click on **Banded Report** again and choose revalidate. Refer to the following screenshot:

We should see that we now have a working report.

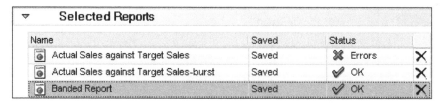

Bulk updating reports

In the **Find/Replace** module, we can perform these same fix options but in bulk. The first way that we can do this is through the option that says **Load Framework Manager Project**, as shown in the following screenshot:

By selecting this option, we are prompted to select a Framework Manager model. We will select the one where I made changes previously, which is `gosales_goretailers.cpf` as shown in the following screenshot:

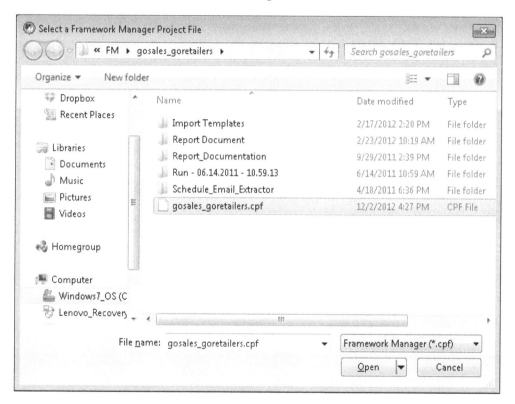

In the next screen, **Global Name Changer** will allow us to select which changes from our model we would like to import. We will leave them all and select **Import** as shown in the following screenshot:

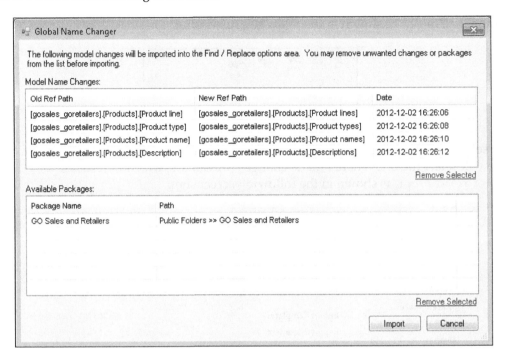

As we do so, what happens on the backend is that MetaManager will run an advanced search path to find all the objects built off the packages in the **Available Packages** area. It will also load the changes as search and replace strings in the bottom section of the module. Refer to the following screenshot:

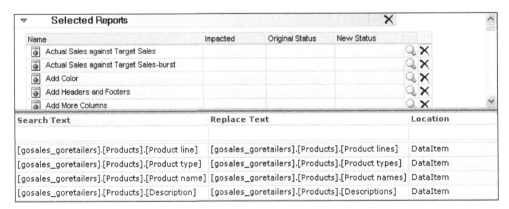

Now we have the option to either press **Preview** or **Update**. **Preview** will allow us to see the impact of our proposed changes before we make them. We can hit **Preview** now to see how making these changes will affect the reports. As you can see, the impacted column will say either **Yes** or **No**; the **Original Status** and **New Status** columns will show up on the impacted reports. The status options are **OK**, **Prompt**, **Errors**, **Warnings**, or **Exception**. Refer to the following screenshot:

Name	Impacted	Original Status	New Status	
Actual Sales against Target Sales	No			🔍 ✕
Actual Sales against Target Sales-burst	No			🔍 ✕
Add Color	Yes	✖ Errors	✔ OK	🔍 ✕
Add Headers and Footers	Yes	✖ Errors	✔ OK	🔍 ✕
Add More Columns	Yes	✖ Errors	✔ OK	🔍 ✕
Associate Columns	Yes	✖ Errors	✔ OK	🔍 ✕
Banded Report	Yes	✖ Errors	✔ OK	🔍 ✕

The description of each status option is as follows:

- **OK**: This status shows that the report is valid and working.

- **Prompt**: This status shows that the report specifications are valid, but there is at least one prompt on the report. If a prompt value is entered that does not meet the criteria of the prompt, the report could still fail.

- **Errors**: This status shows that the report specifications are not valid. If you click on a report and go to the **Details** tab at the bottom, you will see why the report is not a valid report.

- **Warnings**: This status allows the report to show a warning when the validation is run. This may not stop a report from running, but it could deliver unexpected results.

- **Exception**: This is a rare status code that will typically show only if none of the other statuses are true. When Integrated Control Suite is installed in conjunction with MetaManager, this status will show when a report is locked or checked out.

In addition to the automatically populated changes, we can also manually enter search and replace strings in a variety of places within a report. The options for the dropdown on the right-hand side of the search and replace areas include many different available search options; they are as follows:

- **None**: This will not perform the replace function. This option can be used to see an impact analysis.

- **DataItem**: This will search and replace on DataItem objects within the reports only.

- **Drill-Through Item**: This will search and replace on drill-through items within the reports only. This is often used after an environment migration is performed.

- **HTML Item**: This will search and replace on HTML items within the reports only. This is exceptionally helpful during migrations if Javascript is used in the report and if the Cognos BI naming conventions have changed between versions.

- **Image Path**: This will search and replace on the image path within the reports only.

- **Package / Cube Reference**: This will search and replace on package or cube references within the reports. This is very helpful for repointing models to a different package after a migration between environments takes place.

- **Report Expression**: This will search and replace on report expressions within the reports only.

- **Text**: This will search and replace on text items within the reports only.

- **Entire Specification**: This will search and replace on the entire specification of a report.

Applying screen tips to report outputs

If you are using screen tips in your framework manager models and want to populate these onto the actual reports, you can do so using the **Screen Tip Generator** module. This is actually a very simple module. All you do is drag the report that you want to add screen tips to from the navigation tree on the left-hand side to the area on the right-hand side that says **Drag items from the portal tree to this area**. Then you can click on **Preview** or **Update** to either see if the report has query items with screen tips associated with them or to populate those screen tips to the report.

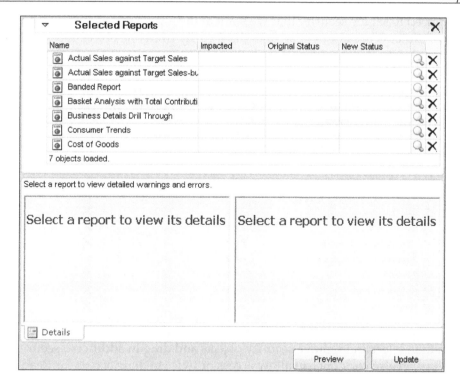

Managing security

There are a few options to update security with MetaManager. The first option is using the **Security Painter** module. This module allows you to update security in bulk on objects, such as reports, report views, packages, folders, or any other Cognos Connection object.

To set the security on a set of objects, we will start by dragging-and-dropping the objects that we want to secure to the bottom section that says **Objects to secure**.

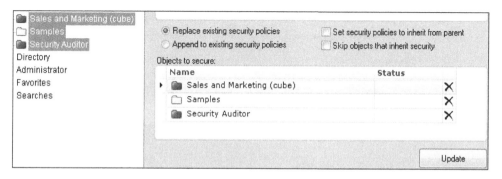

We next need to set the security that we want at the top. The reason they call it **Security Painter** is because we can take the security from one object and paint it onto other objects. We should start with the existing security of another object by dragging that object to the top area. For our example, we are going to drag the **GO Sales and Retailers** package to the top where it says **Security to apply**. When we do so, it will load the security from that **GO Sales and Retailers** model at the top. Refer to the following screenshot:

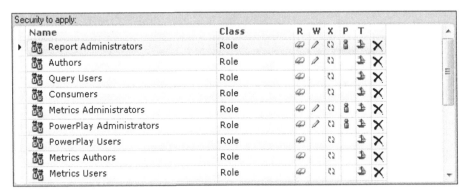

You can then select and remove security objects and drag in additional security items. You can also click once to allow access or twice to deny access for Read(**R**), Write(**W**), Execute(**X**), Set Policy(**P**), and Traverse options(**T**).

If we then hit **Update**, it will apply the security at the top to all of the objects at the bottom.

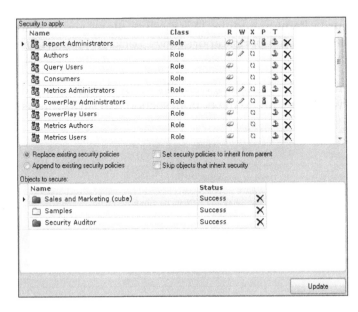

In addition to object-level security, we can update capability, group, and role security using the **Security Editor** extended module that allows for a freeform drag-and-drop of the security into other security objects. We could also replicate security among users or between environments using the **Security Replicator** extended module.

Distributing portal tabs

Portal tab distribution is a key feature of MetaManager. In Cognos BI, portal tabs act as dashboards. The greatest dashboard may have been designed and built, but Cognos BI does not have an easy way to distribute portal tabs to existing customers. That is where the **Pagelet Blasters** module comes into play. Again, this is a very simple module. You can drag users or groups to the bottom. We are going to drag **Administrator** to the bottom from the **Directory** area. We are then going to perform one of the built-in searches. From the `Misc` folder, we shall select **All pagelets in the content store**. This will perform an advanced search path that will bring back all the pagelets that are available in the content store.

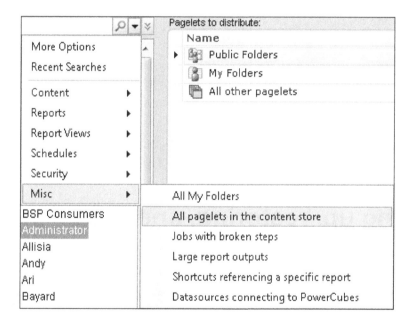

You can then select one or more pagelets to drag to the top section and hit **Update** to push the pagelets to the users at the bottom.

Standardizing headers and footers

Another very simple module is the **Template Blasters** module. This module is used to standardize headers and footers across multiple reports. To do so, find a report that has the headers and footers that you like and drag it to the section that says **Drag & drop source report to this area...** on the right-hand side. For the purpose of our example, we will drag in the **GO Chart** report from the **GO Sales and Retailers** package under the GO Template Samples folder. Next, we will drag in the first two reports from the Report Studio Report Samples folder and press **Update**. Refer to the following screenshot:

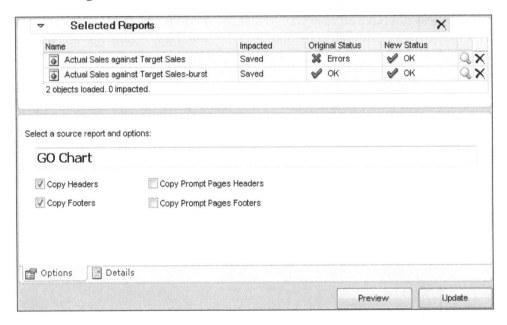

Backing up, restoring, and deploying content

The **Backup / Restore / Deploy** module is designed for content recovery and content deployment. The concepts are simple. As a best practice, you should back up content periodically. Natively in Cognos BI, this is done through the content export section of Cognos administration. The problem with this approach is that it only allows full content restoration. With the MetaManager **Backup / Restore / Deploy** module, you can do complete backups or partial backups. You can also do complete or partial restores and complete or partial deployments.

You can get into the **Backup / Restore / Deploy** module from any of the other modules by clicking on the **Create a backup** button at the top of each module, as shown in the following screenshot:

Once in the module, we will start by creating a backup of some content. While on the **Backup** tab, we will drag in the first 10 reports from the Report Studio Report Samples folder. We will then name our backup location and give the file the name Backup.mmz. We can add comments to the backup as well and then select the option that we want to back up. Refer to the following screenshot:

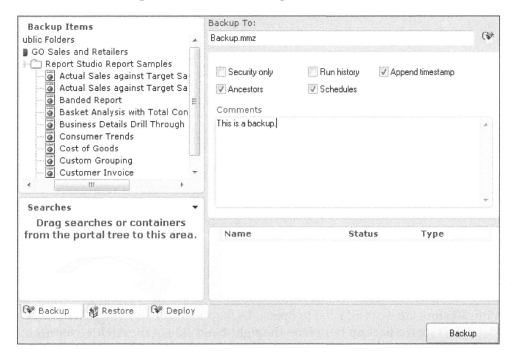

With this module, it is often scheduled so that backups can happen at set times periodically. To schedule the backup, select the save icon in the top-left corner. You will be able to give your saved set of parameters a name with the extension .mmz. You can then use the command line to run the parameters through MetaManager. In addition to this, you can utilize a .bat file to schedule as many .mmz files to run as makes sense in your environment.

For our purposes, we will click on **Backup** to perform the backup now. You will see the names of each object that is being backed up appear in the lower-right section. You will also see the status change for each object being backed up until it reaches a status called **Complete**. Refer to the following screenshot:

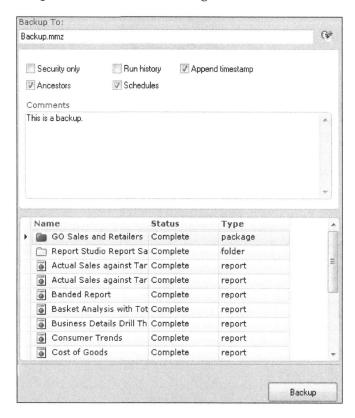

We will next look at restoring objects that have been changed or deleted. To begin with, we will move to the restore section by clicking on the tab at the bottom that says **Restore**.

On this **Restore** tab, we will need to open a backup to begin restoring. To do so, click on the **Open a backup** button on the right-hand side of the **Archive location:** section as shown in the following screenshot:

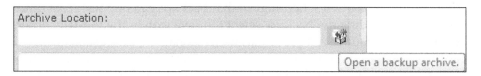

We can then navigate to the backup that we just created to see the contents that were backed up.

 Note that the backup will have a date and timestamp appended to the end if you left that option checked on the **Backup** tab.

To restore an item, simply drag it from the **Archive Content** section to the lower-right drop zone and click on **Restore** as shown in the following screenshot:

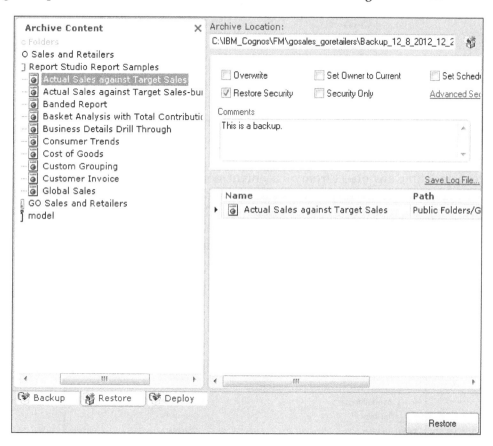

One nice feature that is available here in the **Restore** tab is the ability to deploy archived content to another location. To do so, toggle the drop-down list in the upper-right corner to another environment. For my example, we will toggle from **Development** to **Production**. You can now drag any archived content directly into the environment navigation tree on the far left-hand side and restore the objects to the location you drag to. This will work across environments as well, which is why this is the first deployment capability.

Finally, we will move to the **Deploy** tab where we can perform true deployments. We will re-authenticate to our **Development** environment by selecting it in the drop-down list in the upper-right corner. We will then select the **Production** environment in the drop-down list that is in the middle, to authenticate to it simultaneously as shown in the following screenshot:

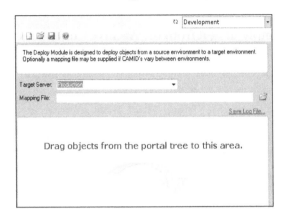

We can now drag any object from our content store to the section in the middle that says **Drag objects from the portal tree to this area**. For the purpose of illustration, we will drag in a report from the **GO Sales and Retailers** package, a pagelet/portal tab, a job, and two datasource connections. When we hit **Deploy**, we will see each object status cycle, from **Adding,** to **Retrieving,** to **Checking,** to **Auditing,** to **Complete**. Refer to the following screenshot:

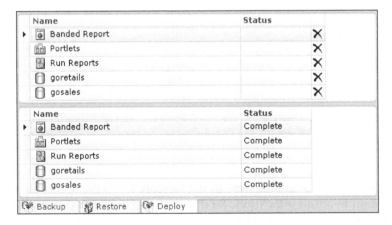

We have now completed a direct deployment. Direct deployments are not possible using IBM Cognos BI natively. Therefore, this is a very worthwhile feature of MetaManager if there is a need to move content between different environments with any sort of frequency.

Documenting content, security, and models

Documentation is valuable in any environment, but there are environments where it is mandatory. Typically, in highly regulated industries such as healthcare or financial industries, there are regulations that require a frequent documentation of mechanisms that are in place for delivering data. MetaManager incorporates documentation around content, security, and models.

Content Documentation

Content documentation is the documentation of anything that lives within your content store. This can be packages, folder structures, reports, security, or datasource connections. It is often critical that this information is captured. MetaManager makes documenting each of these objects very simple using the **Content Store Documenter** module.

Within **Content Store Documenter**, we can drag objects from our content store and drop them in the section that says **Drag objects from the portal tree to this area**. For this example, we can drag in the **GO Sales and Retailers** package. Next, we will need to choose what our output will be. We do this by selecting the folder icon to the right-hand side of where it says **Specify an output file**. Note that we can document to HTML, PDF, XML, or text. If you choose XML, you can also provide an XSL transform file for transforming the XML file after it is rendered. In the middle section, we are able to choose which properties to document and set options for documenting security. The attributes list that is available for documentation includes all attributes stored in the content store. It is freeform to allow you to select the attributes that are most relevant, or you can select all, or select from built-in groups as shown in the following screenshot:

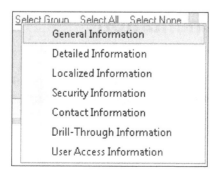

We can now select the document to create our content store documentation. When we document the **GO Sales and Retailers** package to PDF with all attributes selected, we will see a document that is formatted as PDF and shows each attribute beneath each content store object. Refer to the following screenshot:

Add Color (Report)

Public Folders >> GO Sales and Retailers >> Documentation Report Samples >> Add Color

Properties

Parent	Parent	
Ancestors	Public Folders >> GO Sales and Retailers >> Documentation Report Samples >> Add Color	
Creation Time	3/15/2005 2:13:18 PM	
Modification Time	7/5/2012 1:27:28 PM	
Allow Notification	true	
Can Burst	false	
Default Output Format	Default Output Format	
Default Portal Action	run	
Disabled	false	
Display Sequence	0	
Execution Prompt	true	
Hidden	false	
Metadata Model Package	Metadata Model Package	
Name	de en fr ja	Hinzufügen von Farbe Add Color Ajouter de la couleur
Object Class	report	
Options	AdvancedOutput AllowAnnotations Prompt PromptCacheMode SelectionBasedFeatures VerticalElements	false false true none true 20
Package Base	/content/package[@name='GO Sales and Retailers']	
Permissions	Permissions	
Policies	Report Administrators	R WX P T + + + + +

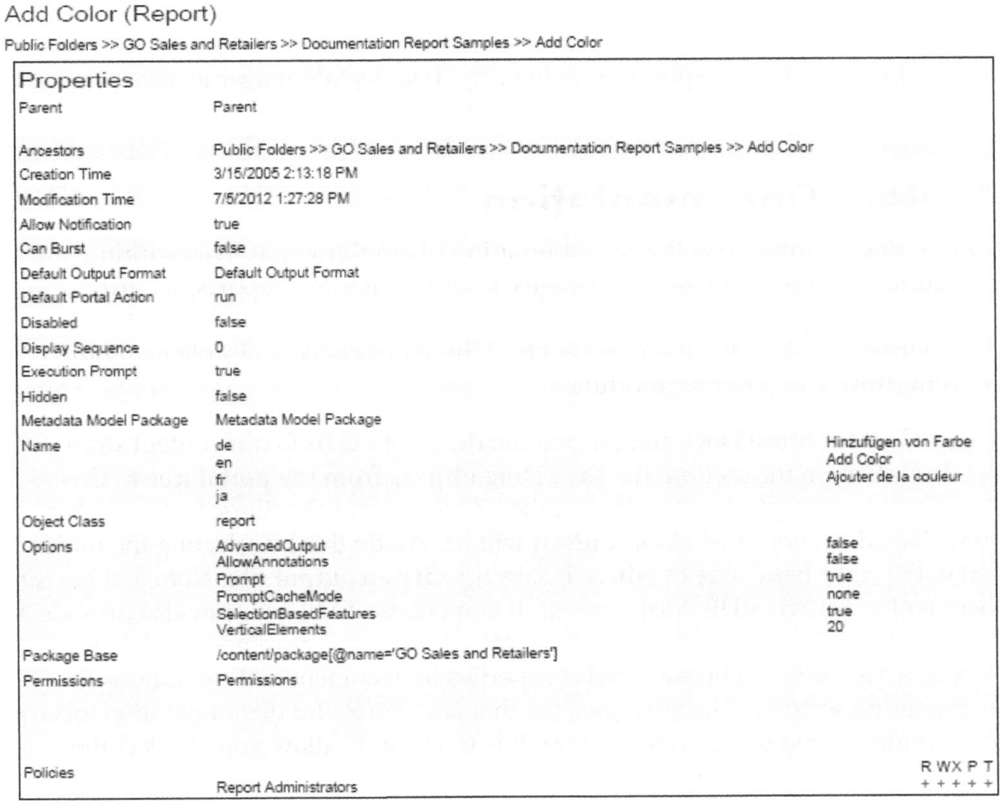

Security Documentation

Most users who utilize **Content Store Documenter** end up using it simply to look at security and access rights. As a result, an additional module was added to MetaManager called **Security Auditor**. **Security Auditor** takes only the security information from the content store and allows you to dump that information to either a delimited text file, Microsoft SQL server, or Oracle, by selecting **Delimited Text File**, **Microsoft SQL Server**, or **Oracle** respectively as shown in the following screenshot:

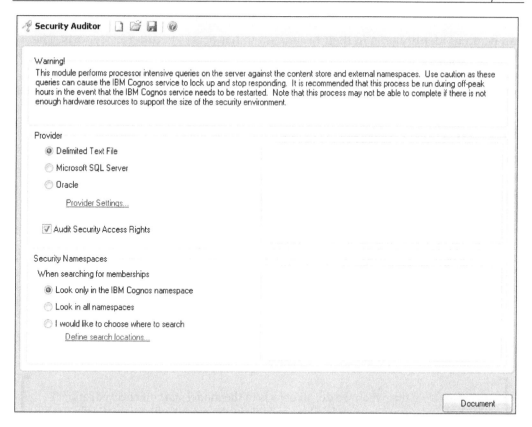

MetaManager ships with a Framework Manager model that you can then point to the newly created datasource, and a set of reports that allow you to report on your security environment. The reports included show things such as who has access to what objects and which users are in which groups. Refer to the following screenshot:

With this module, companies that require strict regulations around access rights can begin to identify who in their organization has access to different reports. The documentation of this security information to a reportable format can be done on a scheduled basis, and by incorporating IBM Cognos BI scheduling, you can have reports automatically send out updates with security information on a periodic basis.

Model documentation

The final piece of documentation that we will look at is model documentation. MetaManager's Model Documenter allows us to document all attributes of a Framework Manager model to HTML, PDF, Excel, or text. With this module, we will first open a model by clicking on the folder icon beside where it says **Select a model file** as shown in the following screenshot:

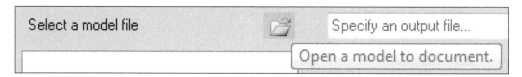

We can now navigate and open the `gosales_goretailers.cpf` model file.

> Note that when we do, all objects in the model start off checked, and all languages or other locales available in the model will automatically load and highlight to the right-hand side under **Filter Locales**.

We can choose **Select None** from the bottom below the locales and then reselect only **en (English)**. We can then choose **Select All** to select all of the options under **Filter Attributes** so that we can document all the attributes of the model. Finally, we can name our documentation file by selecting the folder icon to the right-hand side of the area that says **Specify an output file**. Refer to the following screenshot:

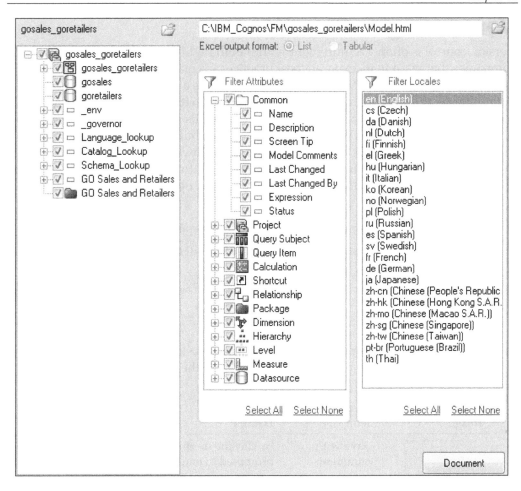

We can now select the document to capture all of the attributes and locales selected for all of the objects to the file format chosen. Since this is traversing an XML file, this documentation is extremely fast and easy to do live. However, it can also be scheduled using the save icon at the top.

Versioning content

Version control is often a requirement within both highly regulated industries and companies that want to incorporate best practices for maintaining their reporting systems. Unfortunately, IBM Cognos BI does not have a way of versioning content out of the box. Integrated Control Suite is a product that was designed for versioning content both inside and outside of IBM Cognos BI. This is a patented solution that is owned and distributed by Avnet (IBM's largest distributor worldwide). Integrated Version Control is a product within this suite that allows the versioning of all objects in the content store, and it has been fully integrated into Cognos Connection. It does so by seamlessly adding additional icons to the IBM Cognos BI studios. Refer to the following screenshot:

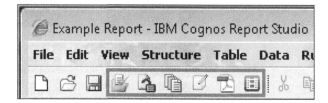

Each new icon or button serves a specific purpose. The key thing to note here is that the buttons look like part of IBM Cognos BI and therefore can be implemented seamlessly for end users.

Image	Icon	Details
	Save with comments	By clicking on this button, you will be prompted to enter information about the version you are saving. You can write comments, add a change control number, or flag the version for deployment to another environment.
	Lock Report	By clicking on this button, you will lock the report you are editing so that no one else can save the report until you complete your updates and unlock the report. This icon will toggle to a locked image once selected. In addition to this, if anyone opens a locked report, Integrated Control Suite broadcast messaging feature will alert the user that the report is locked.

Image	Icon	Details
	View Revision History	By clicking on this button, you will be brought to a list of all saved versions. You can read or update version comments, compare various versions, promote versions, or compare versions to those that are available in other environments.
	Toggle Sticky Notes	By clicking on this button, you will open a sticky note that will allow you to add a comment on the report for other developers. This note cannot be seen when the report is rendered. It is only viewable within the studio.
	Document Report	By clicking on this button, you will create a PDF documentation of the report. This documentation will capture prompt, query, and object information from the report.
	Watch the ICS Video Tutorial	By clicking on this button, you will launch Integrated Control Suite tutorial videos.

In addition to the capabilities available within the studios, there are tons of features that are added to the administration area for maintaining Integrated Control Suite. Each feature available can be secured so that only certain users will have access to any given feature. You can also customize the labels and design of how the tool is implemented into your environment. A complete documentation from BSP Software is available with this tool. You can read more about it at `http://www.BSPSoftware.com`.

Archiving content outputs

Archiving is also available within Integrated Control Suite as a tool called Integrated Archive Service. This is a tool that runs on the backend so that end users are oblivious to its existence. It is used to shrink the size of growing content stores.

The problem is that IBM Cognos BI is designed in a way that utilizes the same database for storing both outputs (that is, Excel or PDF outputs from saved report runs) and application settings (that is, what objects are rendered on each screen, what objects are in which folders, and which services to use for each part of the application to run). A more logical solution would have been to separate these two functions. What happens is that as the content store grows with report outputs, activities such as folder navigation start to slow down because the database that is being used is just too big.

With Integrated Archive Service, stored outputs are moved to a separate database. The end result is that the content store size shrinks substantially and IBM Cognos BI's performance improves drastically. This feature can be scheduled to search for new content and to synchronize completely at regular intervals. You can also select what content to archive if you do not want to archive all the content. Additionally, you can force an archive to be generated manually.

Retrieving deleted content

We looked at using MetaManager for retrieving deleted content with the **Backup / Restore / Deploy** module. Within Integrated Control Suite, there is also a tool for retrieving deleted content. It is called Integrated Recycle Bin. Much like a recycle bin that is utilized in many operating systems, Integrated Recycle Bin allows an end user to restore deleted content from the **My Recycle Bin** area of Cognos Connection. We looked briefly at the end user interface for this in *Chapter 1, IBM Cognos Connection*. With Integrated Recycle Bin, the Cognos administrator will also have an interface where they can restore content globally. As an administrator, one can say where to store deleted content, how often to purge deleted content, and view deleted content globally for all users or on an individual user basis.

Within the administration area of Integrated Recycle Bin, an administrator can restore deleted content or empty the recycle bin.

The business case for add-on tools

Add-on tools are typically developed to fill gaps that were left during the original development of a product. The tools discussed in this chapter are no different. IBM Cognos BI is one of the leading tools in the industry for business intelligence, but no tool is perfect. One of the common concerns brought up by customers has always been around the administration interfaces. MetaManager addresses that concern by creating a single interface for performing administration tasks across multiple environments. It was purpose-built based on feedback from a variety of large and small IBM Cognos customers. Additionally, Integrated Control Suite was designed to meet governance, risk, and compliance requirements that exist in many industries and within publicly traded companies.

So, why should you consider spending more than you already have? MetaManager is going to decrease the time that it takes for Cognos administrators to do their jobs. It will also allow your administrators to do things that they are not able to do natively within Cognos BI. The end result will be more time for administrators to repurpose on more value-adding activities. You will also find that you are able to do things that you could not have otherwise done. Documentation, for instance, is something that is often overlooked or done halfway. Because documentation takes so long, it can be a huge time drain, and in turn, a huge cost that gets added to a Cognos BI project. With MetaManager, documentation can be performed more frequently with little to no user interaction. In essence, MetaManager allows you to automate much of your administration tasks and guarantees accuracy through programmatically performing these tasks.

Integrated Control Suite tends to be a more difficult tool to show a return on investment on, unless there is a project already underway to improve source control within your reporting environment. When you start to compare having a fully integrated, automatic source control option to having to manually version everything, it is very easy to show a return on investment. If that project does not yet exist, it is very likely that it will, as more regulations develop among each industry.

Summary

In this chapter, we looked at add-on tools that have been designed for streamlining and automating the administration of IBM Cognos BI. We also looked at a suite of tools designed to meet regulatory requirements around the versioning of reporting systems. We explored the interfaces for each product so that we could better understand how to use each once they have been implemented. We addressed all the needs of administrators, from content validation to documentation. We also looked at how utilizing such tools could be beneficial to the business.

In the next chapter, we are going to take a step back from technical requirements and look at practical ones around implementing a reporting system. We will begin to explore how to create better user adoption of the technology that we have invested in to enable us to make the most of that investment.

12
User Adoption

This chapter will cover the most important step to a successful implementation, that is, user adoption. In the movie The Field of Dreams, Kevin Costner's character continued to see the aberration of a baseball player who would say, "If you build it, they will come". The reality is, that may only be true in the movies. Adapting a new technology is really quite simple, but that is only until the users get involved. If only we could build out our perfect Cognos BI environment like the one that we see in all of the demos, magically all of the users would flock to it. Unfortunately, in reality, user adoption is never that simple. Unlike technology, there is no manual or guide to user adoption. Most of us work in an environment where IT and business are quite separate. In these types of environments, there is a huge disconnect. This can manifest itself as simple issues such as who pays for this technology?, or more complex issues such as who owns this technology and who is responsible for its success? I want to address practical ways for an IT group implementing Cognos BI to increase user adoption and gain business buy-in.

In the Cognos BI world, you can build the greatest reporting system ever, but without taking the proper steps, user adoption will never take place. That is why we are going to spend an entire chapter just looking at how to encourage user adoption. The technical aspects of IBM Cognos BI can be perfect, but without the users buying in to the new implementation, your new business intelligence initiative will fail.

In this chapter, we will look at:

- The first step – executive sponsorship
- How to build an internal user community (BICC, BICoE)
- Why the right development team matters
- How to partner with IBM and the partner community

- Feedback and its role in the development process
- How training is the key to success
- The business case for user adoption

The beginning – executive sponsorship

Everyone knows that direction for an organization comes from the top. It is no different when implementing a new reporting system. Therefore, the first step to success is always going to be to find an executive sponsor.

You may be wondering how to identify the right executive. You could be afraid about how you would approach an executive and ask about something like this. You could even be concerned that business intelligence is not something that your executives are thinking about. The truth is that these are all valid concerns. My best advice is simply to listen. According to recent research, most executives are concerned with being able to make faster, better-informed decisions. What they may not know is that business intelligence is the solution that allows them to do so.

By listening within your organization, you will start to hear these things come up. If you do hear something related to data not translating to information well enough, that is your cue. You can begin to explain that business intelligence is the way that an organization can take the data it collects and convert it into information for making decisions.

You should also not be afraid to ask for an executive sponsor. If your company has decided that a business intelligence initiative is going to take place, you should ask the executives which one of them has the most pressing need for more, accurate information. Chances are good that you will have a few volunteers.

Once you identify the right executive sponsor, you should start to develop a plan for how you can bring more information to their fingertips. Most executives have at least heard of the concept of an executive dashboard. An executive dashboard is a summarized view of information that is relevant to an executive. This may be the high-level financials per region for a CFO or it could be something more extensive, such as top customers and top suppliers for a COO. As a consultant, I always liked to start a new initiative with an executive dashboard. Why? Because once an executive has meaningful information, they start to want more. Once they have more, they want the people that report to them to have more. Once they have more, they want their employees to have more. And so on, and so forth until business intelligence permeates throughout an organization.

The reality is that a top-down approach like this leads to a better-implemented solution. The numbers that are put together at each level have to roll up to the numbers at the top, and suddenly we see organizations making decisions from concrete information at each and every level, rather than making decisions based on gut instincts or assumptions that are often not true.

In addition to being able to push the business intelligence initiative down the ladder from the top, executives also hold the purse strings and are able to cover the costs of a new initiative. If you start developing business intelligence in silos within your organization, some of the valuable outputs may make their way to the management, but possibly not enough to justify the spend in their eyes. For example, if an executive has approved a spend of $1,000 to develop an executive dashboard, and they see tons of new information as a result, which helps them to perform their jobs better, it is easy to justify that spend. On the other hand, if an executive approves spending that same $1,000 for a department to develop a report that makes that department more efficient, it is much more difficult for the monetary results of that spend to be visible to the executive. As a result, you risk losing the funding to continue development.

So, in summary, not only should you find the executive that is willing to sponsor the business intelligence project, but you should make them your first internal customer as well.

Building an internal user community

Before we dive into building an internal user community, we should look at defining what an internal user community is. Within the IBM Cognos BI community, there are external user groups. These are typically groups of IBM Cognos BI users from different companies that are geographically based and meet periodically to discuss how each company is using IBM Cognos BI. An internal user community is very similar, but they are all from the same company, and they often contain full-time roles that are designed for supporting the overall business intelligence initiative. These groups are often called **Business Intelligence Competency Centers (BICCs)** or **Business Intelligence Centers of Excellence (BICoEs)**.

A common misperception is that BICCs and BICoEs are only needed in extremely large companies with thousands of IBM Cognos BI users. The reality is that a BICC or BICoE would add value to any environment.

So, why are these internal user communities so important? There are a few reasons. One main reason is that they allow users in the forum to discuss what is going well and what is not going well. They also facilitate and encourage new thoughts and new innovations within the space. They provide a way for end users to share what they are looking for in future development with the business intelligence teams that are doing the development. They also allow end users to feel that they have a voice. I have found that simply giving end users a voice to share how they feel and what they want is one of the biggest steps toward user adoption. The interesting thing is that you do not even have to give them what they want in order for it to help. All you have to do is allow them to share and show that you are sympathetic to their wishes. I'll share an example. I was working for a large insurance company, and we were rolling out a new version of Cognos BI company-wide to thousands of users. Many of these users had been using the old version of Cognos BI for over 10 years. When we announced that we would be taking away their old versions of Cognos BI, they simply were not happy. So, we set up a series of meetings with each group, as we were leading them through the transition. In almost every session, someone from each group would ask if they could stay on the old version and explain why it would be better for them if they could. That left us with only a few choices. We could let them stay on a version of Cognos BI that was soon not going to be supported any longer. Alternatively, we could tell them that we did not care about their concerns and they had to move, or we could show them that we did care and help them through the transition. We chose the third option. The end result was that we were able to identify the reports that many users were afraid of losing, migrate those reports to the new system, and teach our users how to access them in the new system. In our scenario, staying on the old system was not an option. However, we still had a choice on how we would treat our user community. By providing them a forum to voice their concerns and addressing rather than ignoring their concerns, we were able to create happy end users.

Another approach that we took during that same implementation was to start with a pilot group. I am a huge advocate for this approach, because it gives you an opportunity to learn through the entire implementation process but on a smaller scale. We saw already that the first project should be with executives. The second project should be with a group of known users. In general, it is a good idea to start small when bringing in a new technology, and that stands true for introducing those new technologies to user communities as well. You may have a grand vision of rolling out Cognos BI company-wide to 5,000 users, but if you try to push it out to all 5,000 at once, you are dooming yourself to fail.

However, if you start with a small group of your users (and I recommend starting with an easy group of known users) and roll Cognos BI out to them, you are doing a few very important things such as building internal advocates, developing processes for rolling out on a larger scale, and increasing the likelihood of user adoption. Once your initial pilot group is successful, their excitement about their new technology will start to spread and permeate through the rest of the organization.

To build an internal user community, you also need a means of bringing them together. An idea that I have seen in some of the larger implementations I have worked on is the development of an internal web page with information about the new technology being rolled out. While we are specifically speaking about Cognos BI here, an internal site could be effective in the unveiling of any new technology. At one of my clients, we provided a very basic website that had a simple calendar, a frequently asked questions page, and a contact form for questions or concerns. Because the site I was working at had a very large user base, we determined that it was best to implement the new Cognos BI technology in phases, and provided key dates for each group of users and their rollouts. If you are working in an established Cognos BI environment, a site like this could be used to provide a forum for asking and answering questions about Cognos BI and for coordinating your internal user group meetings.

The right development team matters

Somewhat related to the creation of a BICC or BICoE is the need to choose the right team to lead your internal business intelligence initiative. What often happens is organizations take purely technical people and put them on business intelligence.

In reality, business intelligence is more than just technical. You absolutely need technical skills to be an effective member of a business intelligence team, but you also need a business aptitude and a personality that works well in front of others. The best members of a business intelligence team will be able to walk the thin line between the technology groups and the business groups. What often happens in any organization is that business groups do not really understand all of the effort and energy that goes into keeping technology running. You will see business managers asking for information that simply is not available in the data or that is very difficult to get to within the data. Similarly, technology teams will not understand the business well enough to know what information is really relevant and will make people's jobs easier. That is where the business intelligence team should come in. We should be able to bridge that gap and understand both the needs of the business as well as the technical requirements to meet those needs.

Sadly, what we see in most organizations is that business intelligence is lumped in with technology, and as such, technical people are added to the teams, and the gap is never bridged. In these types of scenarios, you typically see very project-based implementations where a business will want a certain report and the business intelligence team will simply be developers of the technology. Unfortunately, this is not making the most of Cognos BI.

To make the most of Cognos BI, you want to have a team of people who can be thoughtful leaders on how to present the most meaningful information. The business intelligence team should be experts in your business, in data visualization, and in the Cognos BI technology. New dashboards and reports should be born from within the team and not based on project-based requirements. When projects are necessary, the business intelligence team should be helping to define the scopes, not simply implementing. This is how a well-formed business intelligence team will work. We should be business analysts and not only developers.

How to partner with IBM and the partner community

So, what happens when your business intelligence team does not look the way I just described? That is where partners and IBM consultants come in. Within the consulting community, we all aspire to be the kind of resource that I have just described. The reality is that very few organizations have more than one or two people who are able to understand the business and the technology. Thus, enter consultants.

There are a few reasons why you would want to consider partnering with IBM or a consulting firm. The first is for very focused projects. Perhaps you are interested in rolling out a new executive dashboard using IBM Cognos Workspace (formerly IBM Cognos Business Insight). Since the technology is so new, you would have to send a team of your internal users for training, just to give them a basic understanding. Alternatively, you could bring in a group of consultants to create the new dashboard and provide your internal team with hands-on training in the process. From a cost and time perspective, this is a far better approach. A further reason you would want to partner on focused projects is because they distract your internal team from their normal jobs. Most organizations do not have teams of developers sitting around waiting for new projects to come in. That is why you partner with consultants. Having a consulting company work for 16 weeks a year, instead of paying a full-time employee for around 52 weeks but who works for those same 16 weeks is more cost-effective.

A second reason to partner is for license purchases. This relates more to partnering with a company that resells the vendors' software. Partners are often able to better negotiate discounts for clients, because they negotiate with any given vendor more frequently. They are also able to further provide discounts by reducing the price from within their margin. In addition, they can help clients to better understand the complexities of licensing. A key thing to note here is that all partners are not created equally. There is a strong tendency for partners to collaborate with the company whose products are being sold. This can come across as a way of strong-arming clients during negotiations. You want to find a partner that is clearly not getting along with vendor during the pricing discussions on your behalf. If they are getting along too well, then they are probably collaborating to get the best deal for themselves and the vendor, and not for you and your company. At the same time, the partner is not going to do anything to hurt their long-term relationship with the vendor. A good partner should be a good partner to both the client and the vendor. They should be the dealmaker that helps to find the right price that the client can afford and that the vendor can accept.

So, how do you find the right partner? The right partner will be honest. They will tell you how things are even if it is not easy. The right partner will be someone that you trust when you talk to them. The right partner will be your trusted advisor. You will know that you are working with a good partner, because they will answer the tough questions. They will be your advocates during discussions with the vendor and they will help you accomplish your business goals as if they were their business goals. So, the same question again, how do you find the right partner? Talk to other companies that are using Cognos BI in your area. There is a good chance that they have one that they like or one that they do not like. You can also ask your IBM representative. Despite the fact that a good partner will have tension with any given vendor, they should also be clearly respected by that same vendor.

So, how do you know if you are not working with the right partner? You should be concerned if you do not trust your partner. You should be even more concerned if your partner does not trust you. A good partner will give you all of the information they have. I have seen many partners play both sides of a negotiation. They will hear a vendor representative say that they can discount to X, but then they will tell their client a higher number, or they will hear from a client that they want to get to a certain price and then they will tell the vendor that exact price. A good partner will keep your interests during negotiations and will not try to only increase a deal size so that they or their company will make more money or get more recognition. In regards to user adoption, you need a partner with an experience of driving user adoption in similar environments to your own. A good partner will be able to help you address user concerns before they arise. A good partner should also be able to have meaningful conversations with the business users that the key people on your team should be able to have as well.

So, why partner, when you can hire? I think there is a time for using a consultant and a time for hiring. The reality is that many of the best resources in the Cognos BI space have moved to being consultants, because there is more money in it. There are still many very capable Cognos BI people within the business, but they are much more few and far between. That is why you should utilize consultants for high-value projects. When you get ready to roll out a big, key initiative, use a consulting company that has done it before. It will be worth the money, and you are likely to deliver a better solution in less time. Conversely, you should not use a consulting company for low-value projects. Often, we see large organizations using our consultants for staff augmentation. As a consultant, I hate to say this, but it is not the best use of your company's money. If you are going to do staff augmentation for report development, you should look for people at a much lower rate than most IBM Cognos BI consulting companies demand. On the other hand, if you need someone that has a lot of experience and who can drive requirements, use a trusted consulting company.

Feedback and its role in the development process

End users need to have a voice throughout development. The first and possibly most important requirement in gaining user adoption is to give your end users a voice. Many businesses have embraced an approach where the business pays for new technology, thus giving them the ultimate voice, the yay or nay decision. While this is an effective way to increase user adoption from the onset, it also adds additional issues preventing what may be a best fit for the company and often creates a void where enterprise-wide solutions would best reside.

A more sensible way then to give your users a voice might be to provide a weekly vent session. When working at the large health insurance company, we provided weekly user meetings while undergoing our migration. As I mentioned, many of the people we were migrating had been working with the old technology for over 10 years, and needless to say, were very reluctant to give it up. By providing them an outlet to voice their concerns, we prevented the negative grapevine effect and were able to smoothly walk people through the migration process. As a result, we had advocates spreading a positive message through the grapevine rather than opposition spreading the negative. Essentially, by creating an internal user group, we accomplished two goals; we provided the end users a voice and we, as the IT organization, gained a better insight into the concerns and goals of our user community.

An important thing to note is that these feedback sessions should be productive, but they should not extend projects beyond their original scope. In the consulting world, we call this scope creep. It is very common for a project to grow as it is being delivered, and this often causes projects to go over budget. Therefore, it is important to sit down with your end users and define exactly what will be delivered during any particular project or phase of a project. You should then set up weekly status meetings where you review where you, as the developer, are in the process. You can also review specific deliverables and try to get a sign off. It is crucially important that if any new requirement comes up, it is identified as a new requirement and an additional budget is allocated for providing it. Alternatively, new requirements should be sidelined for future phases of a project. Not calling these out as they arise result in projects that run long or over budget. Remember that feedback is a two-way communication. While your end users should be providing feedback to you on how your development efforts are going, you should also be providing open and honest feedback as issues arise.

One area that many development teams struggle with is addressing issues head on. It is very common for a project to come to a planned end only to find out that there are many undelivered deliverables. Most of the time, these are not issues that have suddenly come up but are issues that came up throughout the project. In the weekly status meetings, you should identify issues that have come up during the week and either work towards a solution or remove the effected deliverables. The last thing that any project should have is surprise. Everything will not go perfectly in every implementation, but that does not give anyone an excuse to not communicate the issues to the business users that are sponsoring the project.

Training is the key to success

The last area of user adoption that we shall discuss is training. A well-trained end user is a happy end user. Many companies spend thousands and thousands of dollars on IBM Cognos BI software, then thousands and thousands more on implementing the software, and then they turn it over to an untrained user community. The sad reality is that they wonder why their newest software solution is not being utilized. People need to be trained. IBM Cognos BI is a very user-friendly piece of business intelligence software. However, businesses still need to take the time and invest the money in training their users. Not doing so would be like building a multi-million dollar professional football field and then sending a group of untrained junior high football players to play on it. It would not make sense.

If you are going to invest the money in the software and the implementation, you should invest the money in your people as well. That is what training is and why it is key to user adoption. It is investment in people. The people that you want to have using your IBM Cognos BI software want to see that you are willing to help them to be successful in doing so.

I recommend coming up with a custom training plan to fit your environment. At the minimum, you want to train your administrators to implement best practice administration methods. You should also spend the money to provide Report Studio training to your developers. When you get to end users, it is debatable whether or not training is required. Many companies choose not to train end users due to the high cost of doing so. In most environments, around 90 percent of your users are Cognos consumers or enhanced consumers that only run reports or may schedule reports to run or interact with a Workspace dashboard. These users should be trained or your company is wasting the investment they have made in their licenses.

The question then comes up, are there less-expensive ways to train a large user base? The answer is yes. The default way to provide training is to send your administrators, developers, and end users for training at an IBM facility. These training classes are great, but they can be very expensive. I recommend that it is best to provide classroom -based training for your administrators and your developers, but that you utilize **computer-based training** (CBT) for your end users. In addition, you can organize for a training class to be conducted onsite at your facility either through IBM or through a partner for a fraction of the cost of sending your developers and administrators to the other training classes that are available. The end result is that you will be better utilizing your investment in the software by investing in your people, and by doing so in a smart way, you can be more cost-effective.

The business case user adoption

It feels kind of weird to write a business case for user adoption, because the users are typically the business people. With that said, it is actually a pretty easy business case to write. If we were running a line of business, and we had just shared in the investment to add a business intelligence tool, we would want to be trained. Chances are good that we have seen the marketing for IBM Cognos BI and seen some demos of how great the final reports or dashboards can look, but we want to understand how do we get to that information. If we are going to be developing basic reports, how do we do so? More importantly, we want the people on our team to be excited about this new investment.

We have made this investment, because we think it is going to improve the way that we do business. We think that it is going to make it easier for employees to make decisions that improve our business. So, we want those people to be excited about using the software. With that in mind, we think business leaders want to see technology that they have invested in to be adopted.

The difficulty in justifying some of the investments in user adoption is that the results are much less tangible. How do you measure user adoption? There are a few ways to do so. One example is through taking end user satisfaction surveys. Alternatively, asking end users questions about how easy the software is to use could help us prove the value of user adoption. Unfortunately, you will never be able to tie user adoption to the bottom line. What you will be able to do, however, is show a better return on your investment in the software by seeing the software more widely used. That alone makes it worth the investment to drive user adoption.

Summary

Finally and in reiteration, we are being provided a lot of information. Each of the points we discussed earlier hits on this position, but the premise is simple; the more we know, the more empowered we feel. After all, knowledge is power, right? Therefore, look for more ways to empower your end users with knowledge. This may manifest itself as a demo or training for the software, the website idea we discussed already, or through internal user group meetings. Regardless of which mechanism you choose, the more your end users are informed, the more likely they are to conform to the new standard you have put in place.

In this book, we have covered both the technical and the business side of IBM Cognos Business Intelligence V10. We have walked through the user interfaces and the development interfaces, as well as reviewed some third-party solutions and the user adoption. Now you are equipped to start utilizing IBM Cognos Business Intelligence V10 fully.

Index

O

objects
  copying 22
  cutting 22
  deleting 22
  pasting 22
Open button 112
Order Information query 218

P

package
  about 12
  publishing 220-222
Page Explorer pane 155
Pagelet Blasters module 263
Palette property 179
Pareto Chart 109
performance tuning
  business case 246
permissions 236
Pie Chart 109
Pivot button 175
Play button 174
Point Chart 109
portal tabs
  distributing 263
Position field 167
Presentation View 221
Prompt button 175
Properties window 36
Public Folders location 87
Publish Wizard 221

Q

Query calculation, object 157
Query Explorer pane 155
query items 72
query subjects 71
Quick Filter
  options 251, 252
Quick tour option 11

R

Radar Chart 109
R&D 63
Redo button 112
repeater table, object 157
report objects
  validating 254-256
reports
  bulk updating 257-259
  running 17, 19, 21
  saving 87
  scheduling 21
  sharing 87
reports outputs
  screen tips, applying 260
report types, Cognos Report Studio
  Active Report 153
  blank 152
  Blank Active Report 153
  chart 152
  crosstab 152
  financial 152
  list 152
  map 152
  Repeater Table 153
report views
  creating 22, 23
request routing
  routing sets, using 243-245
Research and Development. *See* R&D
Restore tab 266
Rich text item, object 158
right-click menu. *See* drag-and-drop
     interface
right team
  selecting 283
Run button 112

S

Save as button 112
Save button 112
Search button 112

Thank you for buying
IBM Cognos Business Intelligence

About Packt Publishing

Packt, pronounced 'packed', published its first book "Mastering phpMyAdmin for Effective MySQL Management" in April 2004 and subsequently continued to specialize in publishing highly focused books on specific technologies and solutions.

Our books and publications share the experiences of your fellow IT professionals in adapting and customizing today's systems, applications, and frameworks. Our solution based books give you the knowledge and power to customize the software and technologies you're using to get the job done. Packt books are more specific and less general than the IT books you have seen in the past. Our unique business model allows us to bring you more focused information, giving you more of what you need to know, and less of what you don't.

Packt is a modern, yet unique publishing company, which focuses on producing quality, cutting-edge books for communities of developers, administrators, and newbies alike. For more information, please visit our website: www.packtpub.com.

About Packt Enterprise

In 2010, Packt launched two new brands, Packt Enterprise and Packt Open Source, in order to continue its focus on specialization. This book is part of the Packt Enterprise brand, home to books published on enterprise software – software created by major vendors, including (but not limited to) IBM, Microsoft and Oracle, often for use in other corporations. Its titles will offer information relevant to a range of users of this software, including administrators, developers, architects, and end users.

Writing for Packt

We welcome all inquiries from people who are interested in authoring. Book proposals should be sent to author@packtpub.com. If your book idea is still at an early stage and you would like to discuss it first before writing a formal book proposal, contact us; one of our commissioning editors will get in touch with you.

We're not just looking for published authors; if you have strong technical skills but no writing experience, our experienced editors can help you develop a writing career, or simply get some additional reward for your expertise.

IBM Cognos Insight

ISBN: 978-1-849688-46-8   Paperback: 142 pages

Take a deep dive into IBM Cognos Insight and learn how this personal analytics tool can be integrated with other IBM Business Analytics products

1. Step-by-step, how to guide, for installing and configuring IBM Cognos Insight for your needs

2. Learn how to build Financial, Marketing and Sales workspaces in Cognos Insight

3. Learn how to integrate and collaborate with IBM Cognos Business Intelligence

IBM Websphere Portal 8: Web Experience Factory and the Cloud

ISBN: 978-1-849684-04-0   Paperback: 474 pages

Build a comprehensive web portal for your company with a complete coverage of all the project lifecycle stages

1. The only book that explains the various phases in a complete portal project life cycle

2. Full of illustrations, diagrams, and tips with clear step-by-step instructions and real time examples

3. Take a deep dive into Portal architectural analysis, design and deployment

Please check **www.PacktPub.com** for information on our titles

**IBM Cognos Business
Intelligence 10.1
Dashboarding Cookbook**

Working with dashboards in IBM Cognos BI 10.1: Design, distribute, and collaborate

Ankit Garg

IBM Cognos Business Intelligence 10.1 Dashboarding Cookbook

ISBN: 978-1-849685-82-5   Paperback: 206 pages

Working with dashboards in IBM Cognos BI 10.1: Design, distribute, and collaborate

1. Exploring and interacting with IBM Cognos Business Insight and Business Insight Advanced

2. Creating dashboards in IBM Cognos Business Insight and Business Insight Advanced

3. Sharing and Collaborating on Dashboards using portlets

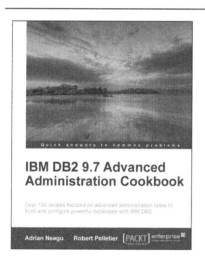

**IBM DB2 9.7 Advanced
Administration Cookbook**

Over 100 recipes focused on advanced administration tasks to build and configure powerful databases with IBM DB2

Adrian Neagu   Robert Pelletier

IBM DB2 9.7 Advanced Administration Cookbook

ISBN: 978-1-849683-32-6   Paperback: 480 pages

Over 100 recipes focused on advanced administration tasks to build and confi gure powerful databases with IBM DB2

1. Master all the important aspects of administration from instances to IBM's newest High Availability technology pureScale with this book and e-book.

2. Learn to implement key security features to harden your database's security against hackers and intruders.

3. Empower your databases by building efficient data configuration using MDC and clustered tables.

Please check **www.PacktPub.com** for information on our titles

Lightning Source UK Ltd.
Milton Keynes UK

9 781849 683562